Praise for Alan Deutschman's

A TALE *of* TWO VALLEYS

"As frothy as La Jolla surf . . . [Deutschman is] a Tom Wolfe to Silicon Valley 'plutocrats,' their pastoral opponents and service employees . . . His tales of rebels in paradise, wealthy weekenders trying to go native, and the 'glassy-winged sharpshooter,' an invasive insect that threatens to suck the water out of the wine, make for a fun read."

—DAVID HELVARG, *Washington Post*

"Just as *Midnight in the Garden of Good and Evil* did for Savannah . . . so does *A Tale of Two Valleys* accomplish for Northern California's wine country: provide an irresistibly witty social history of an intriguing place, largely as viewed through encounters with its most colorful denizens . . . [A] splendidly entertaining book."

—*Santa Fe New Mexican*

"Breezy . . . . informative and fun."   —*Albany Times Union*

"Deutschman . . . has just the r[...]d, and continually bemused . . . Y[...]curacy."

[...]*ng*

"Contrasting the luxurious Napa Valley and its more bohemian cousin Sonoma, Deutschman finds a struggle for the 'soul of a place' . . . An insightful examination of a long-running feud between the haves and have mores."   —*People*

BROADWAY BOOKS

New York

A
TALE
of TWO
VALLEYS

Wine, Wealth, and the Battle for the Good Life
in Napa and Sonoma

Alan Deutschman

A hardcover edition of this book was published
in 2003 by Broadway Books.

PRINTED IN THE UNITED STATES OF AMERICA

BROADWAY BOOKS and its logo, a letter B bisected on the diagonal, are
trademarks of Broadway Books, a division of Random House, Inc.

Visit our website at www.broadwaybooks.com

First trade paperback edition published 2004

Book design by Caroline Cunningham

The Library of Congress has cataloged the hardcover edition as follows
Deutschman, Alan, 1965–
A tale of two valleys : wine, wealth, and the battle for the good life in
Napa and Sonoma / Alan Deutschman.
p. cm.
1. Sonoma Valley (Calif.)—Social life and customs.   2. Napa Valley
(Calif.)—Social life and customs.   3. Sonoma Valley (Calif.)—Rural
conditions.   4. Napa Valley (Calif.)—Rural conditions.   5. Wine
industry—Social aspects—California—Sonoma Valley.   6. Wine
industry—Social aspects—California—Napa Valley.   7. Wealth—Social
aspects—California—Sonoma Valley.   8. Wealth—Social aspects—
California—Napa Valley.   9. Social conflict—California—Sonoma Valley.
10. Social conflict—California—Napa Valley.   I. Title.
F868.S7 D48 2003
979.4'18—dc21
2002026248

ISBN 0-7679-0704-3

1 3 5 7 9 10 8 6 4 2

To my parents, as always,

and to Susan

for the best day I spent in Sonoma

CONTENTS

PREFACE

The Plague in Paradise

THE PLAGUE WAS COMING.

The carrier was a flying parasitical insect. Death with wings. It was hardly noticeable, only a half-inch long and nearly transparent. But it spread a bacterial disease.

An epidemic. Incurable. Fatal.

The people would be unharmed, in body at least, but their cherished lands would be ravaged. Tens of thousands of acres. The most valuable crop in the world. The source of the great wealth of the two valleys and their extraordinary power over the imagination of the American nation.

The insect would pierce the vines with its mouthpiece and suck out a thousand times its own weight in liquid as it tried to find the nutrients it needed from within the plant. It would excrete the excess water in a continuous stream, as though it were a powerful sprinkler irrigating the fields.

After it had sucked out what it wanted, the ungrateful parasite killed its host. The bug maliciously prevented the plant from feeding itself. The pest left behind a bacteria inside the vine that blocked it from drawing water from its roots and up through its cane to nourish the hanging fruit.

The vine would slowly die of thirst in the sun.

The thick canopies of green leaves would burn to yellow and then brown. The clusters of grapes would wilt and dry.

The earth would be scorched.

The plague was coming but an outsider would not have understood that many of the inhabitants of the two valleys thought this was good.

Some thought it furtively and some whispered it at the coffee shop and the town square and others said it aloud in the town hall meetings and the newspapers.

The plague was coming and some of the natives thought that their neighbors had brought it upon themselves. They had invited devastation by their avarice and pride. They had torn out nearly everything else to make way for the cash crop that was worth billions of dollars every harvest. They had ripped away the other vegetation that might have served as barriers to the progress of the insect or provided habitats for rival creatures that preyed on the invader. They had defied nature and now they were witnessing its retribution. They had the hubris to overturn the natural order of rampant biological diversity, but now the planet was restoring its own balance. Evolution was striking back with this killer insect, a mutation that was deadlier to the vines than any that came before. Humans had thought that they could impose their will on the environment, but now they would be humbled and humiliated by forces far more powerful than themselves.

The plague was coming. The deadly insect, *Homalodisca coagulata*, popularly called the "glassy-winged sharpshooter," was carrying the bacteria *Xylella fastidiosa*. The apocalyptic messenger had already destroyed vast acreages of vineyards in the southern reaches of the state. The names of those places were far less well-known, but the devastation was as a solemn warning. The people here knew that their lands were next.

The plague might be stopped. The activists warned their fellow residents that the government was quietly developing a plan. Pesticides sprayed from above. Airplanes flying low over the valleys. Chemicals could kill the insect. Nerve toxins. Proven carcinogens. Substances that could harm not only the insects but also the citizens and their children in their homes and gardens and schoolyards near the farmlands.

A choice had to be made, they said. Profits or people. The elite or the masses. It was a reemergence of class warfare. Marx not in the factories of the industrial revolution but in the valleys of an anachronistic agricultural paradise.

Many of the people were secretly wishful that the wine business would be wiped out so that all the rich outsiders, lured there by its legend, would finally leave and the valleys could be reclaimed by the people who had been there *before*. They wanted to force away the new-money invaders. They were fighting to repel them politically. Putting forward their own candidates. Trying to take over city hall. Passing petitions to place voter referendums on the ballot. But even if that didn't work, nature might seek its own mighty revenge, as though the elites deserved a biblical vengeance.

THIS IS A STORY of the struggle for the soul of a place. It is about America's ambivalence over the right ways to preserve or exploit our remaining natural spaces. It's about our quests to live amid scenic beauty without inevitably ruining what attracted us there. It's about the difficulties of sustaining our unique local cultures, with their quirkiness and eccentricities, in this era of a rapidly proliferating and nearly pervasive mass culture. It's about the troubled efforts of people from wildly diverse subcultures to live closely together with civility and even harmony. It's about shifting conceptions of status and privilege in a nation where the cultural legacy is swiftly recast and a powerful new elite is created every generation. It's about seekers of the good life and the inspiration and fervor they bring to their pursuit. It's about the hazards of trying to spend our burgeoning wealth without undermining our humanistic values or provoking a new round of class warfare. And it's about a bunch of admirably impassioned people fighting fiercely over their competing visions of an ideal community.

This particular narrative is set in the wine country of the northern coast of California, a fabled locale with celebrated names—Napa! Sonoma!—but many of the same conflicts are occurring in scores of lesser-known places in every region across our country. The same struggles are playing out within easy driving distance of every encroaching metropolis. The identical issues are arising at embattled rural outposts that until recently were considered safely isolated and too remote for prodigious development. We're at the beginning of a furious debate about the future of our farmlands, our towns, our small communities—the parts of America, still vast, that haven't been homogenized into the conformity of undifferentiated sprawl, sameness, and soullessness.

After making such presumptuous claims to relevance and significance, I must confess that I didn't approach this project with the high intentions of a self-important social critic or the incorrigibility of a do-gooder or even the Olympian detachment of a scholar. My initial motivation was spectacularly hedonistic. It made me the object of an embarrassing amount of undisguised envy among my professional colleagues and friends and cocktail-party acquaintances.

The idea was to live in paradise—*for free*!

To dwell in a place that was famously beautiful and renowned for its extraordinary food and its superlative climate. A place that was extolled by the sumptuous photography and uncritical prose of a cadre of slick magazines as a lifestyle fantasy for both the fabulously affluent and the ambitiously aspiring.

And I could live there—*free!*—because I had a number of generous good friends who were spectacularly rich. Not just doctor-lawyer-banker rich, not just sportscars-in-the-three-car-garage rich, not thrifty-millionaire-next-door rich. No, this was a rarified class that had so many millions that they had to be modified by Greek prefixes: centimillionaires and decamillionaires. These were the kind of people whose outlandish paper wealth was best calculated by consulting mandatory documents filed with the Securities and Exchange Commission.

I had developed lasting friendships with these plutocrats during a decade of chronicling Silicon Valley as a magazine journalist—for *Fortune*, *Gentlemen's Quarterly*, and *Vanity Fair*—and as the author of a biographical book about Steve Jobs, the billionaire cofounder of Apple Computer. They lived near me in San Francisco, but they also owned villas in the wine country of the Napa and Sonoma valleys, a drive of only one to two hours to the north. In the summer, when the city was notoriously foggy and chill, they would invite me up to spend long weekends at their private, secluded enclaves in the intense sunshine and perfect humidity-free eighty-degree-plus temperatures. I would cavort at their estates and stay over in their pool houses.

Their notion of the "pool house" was delightfully comic since those structures were so luxurious and large, hardly the image of diminutive, makeshift shacks that the term implied. Top chefs would have coveted the pool-house kitchens with their wood-burning pizza ovens and their yards of granite countertops. Gearheads would be impressed by the elaborate installations of electronics equipment and the extensive libraries of audio and video recordings.

The pool houses were the Grand Trianons of their latter-day Versailles. Most people would have wanted to live there full time.

Admittedly, I did.

And then I had the realization that I *could* stay at my friends' villas during the weekdays, when they were back in the city making more money. I could ensconce myself in their Trianons or even in the main palaces if I so desired.

I could become a permanent house guest, the Kato Kaelin of the wine country.

And so, in the spring of 2000, I found myself holding duplicate sets of keys to a magnificent mansion on eighty-five acres near the summit of Howell Mountain overlooking the Napa Valley, and to a luxurious ten-acre estate in the foothills of Sonoma Mountain above the Sonoma Valley, and to a perfect cottage on the valley floor in the town of Sonoma, the most historic village in the wine country.

My intentions were innocent enough but foolishly naïve. I thought that with money that I saved on rent, I could indulge lavishly in the lifestyle I had imagined from the magazines. I could live in spectacular natural settings. I could cook with fresh ingredients bought directly from the local organic farmers and cheesemakers and become a regular at the foodie temples and spend afternoons hiking through the hills and relaxing in hot tubs and mud baths and receiving massages. I could get to know the wine people and learn the secrets of their realm.

I did all those things, to be sure. But before long my initial aspirations for guiltless hedonism, sensuality, and voyeurism were impinged by my instincts as a reporter. On the weekends the wine country was peopled with gracious hosts smiling at their overnight guests, but during the weekdays the families feuded with each other and with their neighbors like the legendary Hatfields and McCoys. It turned out that there was deeply rooted trouble in this supposed paradise. There was a cultural civil war in the wine country. And as a newcomer I felt the pressure to pick sides.

The most obvious rift was demarcated by the long high wall of the Mayacamas Mountains, which separate Napa and Sonoma. The Napa Valley had become synonymous with elitism and prestige and the excesses of wealth and hedonism. In the Sonoma Valley, though, the momentum of the money culture was in conflict with an almost anachronistic ideal of rural living and small-town community. Sonoma seemed destined to become the new Napa, but its people were wary of that fate.

So, in the old town of Sonoma, a burgeoning grassroots movement was seizing power and opposing the new-money types, whose trophy houses and proposed luxury hotels threatened to push out the humbler natives as well as the transplanted free spirits and iconoclasts who had created a new bohemia there. The movement's leaders were a combative and brilliantly colorful bunch. They included Ken Brown, a former New York City taxi driver and vineyard grape picker with a waist-length ponytail; Maria "Ditty" Vella, the scion of a four-generation Sicilian-American dynasty that made America's very best cheese; and Tom Whitworth, an Englishman who had quit a career at the heights of the international advertising business to live in a barn surrounded by wild peacocks.

The bohemians were leading a populist revolt, an inspired backlash against the egomania and rapaciousness of the elites. Even though I had come to town as the guest of the new-money invaders, I found myself "going native" as I began identifying more with the bohemians and their causes. I watched as their uprising tried to take control of the local government—and as it ultimately ended with the sudden tragic death of one of the most powerful figures in the valley.

PART I

A Place Unlike

the Rest of

America

THE DENSE, DOGGED TRAFFIC persisted across the Golden Gate Bridge and all through the Marin County suburbs. The freeway's congestion continued for a twenty-mile stretch. Then, as a city dweller, I felt a quiet thrill and a sense of anticipation to see "Sonoma" in reflective letters on the green sign suspended over the roadway. Few place names held a sense of promise in their very sound, the way they did to Proust's narrator as he surveyed a map, but "Sonoma" was one.

The word worked like an incantation, for as I turned off of Highway 101 and swung sharply eastward, the trappings of suburban sprawl disappeared almost instantly. The motels and fast-food drive-throughs and office parks and housing tracts were suddenly banished. There were open fields on either side of the road. It began to feel like the country, but the remnants of modernity were still too near to be certain. A first-time visitor wouldn't be sure whether this was just an anomalous patch that somehow had defied development but would soon give way to the pervasive concrete and neon of homogenous civilization.

Then came the real portal to a radically different place and culture. There was a little bridge over the Petaluma River, which flows north from San Francisco Bay. The water marked the border to Sonoma County. The span had a gentle arc, and as I came to its peak and could see the other side, I was hit by a panorama of spacious pastures, flat and expansive, a purely rural environment. The roadway descended to the ground and I passed lushly green sod farms. I saw grazing fields with hundreds of idly lounging cows.

The Sonoma borderline had an actual meaning; unlike so many place names that had been reduced to little more than arbitrary post-office markings and administrative zones in a vast undifferentiated megalopolis, Sonoma was a pronounced break, an anomaly and anachronism, a place that still defined itself by a lasting heritage of rural and small-town country life.

On the left there was an old decaying red barn. The corrugated metal panels were torn from its pitched roof. The wood siding was cracking and coming undone. A grain tower leaned at a sharp angle, seemingly ready to topple, a homegrown Pisa. It was next to a farmhouse that was so magnificently warped that its shape, once rigidly squared, had turned sensuously curvilinear. These were the kind of buildings that Walker Evans might have photographed for his portraits of the austere beauty of the impoverished South during the Great Depression. What a shock that this scene was so close to the rich technophilic city, hardly thirty miles, and that I had just passed a string of the most expensive suburban towns in America, and that those cows could spend the day snoozing on such prohibitively costly soil, and that this barn hadn't been supplanted by hundreds of houses.

The grazing land extended from the plain into the voluptuous foothills. While the Marin hills were mostly covered by evergreens, here the sculpted earth forms had been denuded in many places to serve as pastures. The surface still had patches of green from the winter's rainy season, when the color was spectacularly vivid. But the dry weeks of April and the intensifying sun had begun to burn the land back to brown.

Outsiders commonly assumed that the "northern" in northern California meant that it's as far up as the Northeast. But the Bay Area actually covered the same latitude as North Carolina, and the spring sun was direct and intense. The local conceit was that the landscape is "green and gold." The greens were ever present, but the rest was still dirty brown to the visitor's eye, an arid, dusty tone rather than a warmly resonant one. The land's beauty was undeniably weird, a little eerie at first, more like an alien planetscape from "Star Trek" than the *Gone With the Wind* conception of country. It was a slowly acquired taste for natives of other climates. But after a few years the sun-scorched surfaces began to seem less like the moon and more like the natural order of things.

This little valley beside the Petaluma River was a geographic vestibule or antechamber, a transition from the people country to the coming entrance to the wine country. It was a chance for city dwellers to decompress and adjust.

The car rose up a little promontory. There was another visual explosion as the Sonoma Valley suddenly appeared, the grand mansion that dramatically opened out of the smaller waiting room. The tableau radiated for thirty miles: the eye followed from south to north, right to left, from the fading waters of the bay toward the marshy wetlands preserves and then the vineyards. I scanned from the foreground of wide-open plains to the far-off backdrop of the Mayacamas, the high, dark curtain of mountains separating Sonoma from Napa.

I swung a sharp left onto Arnold Drive, named for a forgotten general who lived in these parts. The road had just a single lane in each direction but nonetheless qualified as one of the major thoroughfares of the Sonoma Valley. Ahead I saw a bunch of cattle amid the unruly grass. A chain-link fence kept them out of the very first vineyard. The neatly ordered horizontal rows of trellises ascended a knoll to a white-shingled winery that looked like a big house.

The road swerved along the edge of the foothills of Wildcat

Mountain. The scene alternated abruptly between new money and old country. A grand Tuscan villa commanded the top of a hill encircled by canopies of vines. A little farther there was a stunning abundance of yellow and red roses beside the low stone walls that proudly demarcated another wealthy vineyard. Then came an antiquated little airstrip that still had a few creaky old biplanes parked by the road. More ruins of barns again evoked the Walker Evans motif. A cluster of tractors and plows, long abandoned to rust, seemed like weird sculptures in the weeds. A hillside hacienda looked over hundreds of parallel rows of chardonnay and pinot noir. Then just across the street there was Angelo's homemade beef-jerky shack with a gloriously kitschy life-sized statue of a cow poised on the roof.

The smell of shit infused the air. In the city the term "organic" connoted freshness, healthiness, pesticide-free safety, but here it meant the pervasive odor of manure, especially on mornings when a farmer plowed a large plot.

I swerved right at the fuel-stop intersection that the locals call Big Bend, where the roads fork to circumnavigate a thousand acres of farms. Later I swung left and passed Ford's Café, where for decades the local farmers have gathered for breakfast and gossip before dawn, as early as four on summer mornings. Ford himself lived in a trailer home behind the ramshackle diner. A semi truck was parked in the gravel lot.

The lingering stink of shit gave way to a soothing perfume. This road was lined by a wall of eucalyptus, a century old and a hundred feet high, with their layers of curled, peeling barks and their drooping sheets of delicately long, thin leaves. The majestic trees emitted a hypnotically sweet aroma, especially in the moist hours after a sustained winter rainfall, when the air was fully saturated with the deliriously seductive scent. And now, during the rainless months from April to November, when the air was so hot and dry, the eucalyptus were like the wood walls of a perfect sauna, and stepping outside felt like entering a spa.

I went by more vineyards and then the road straightened and a remarkable vista opened suddenly. Far in the distance, down a wide avenue, there was a soaring, slender palm tree in front of the creamy, rough-hewn stone of Sonoma's old city hall. It stood at the center of the verdant town square, the Plaza, which was backed by a high vertical wall of mountains densely covered with green trees. The idea of the natural, curvaceous hills as a curtain behind the linear precision of the manmade vista evoked the aesthetics of refined Old Europe. But as I came closer, the facades of the vintage buildings surrounding the square—weathered stone, craggy adobe, warped wood—were remnants of a raucous cowboy town of the Old West.

I drove along the edge of the Plaza, looking toward the arched canopies of tall trees and the circular stone fountain surrounded by groomed hedges and the vibrantly colorful rose garden. Stopping at the southeast corner, I noticed something most unusual. A healthy, well-fed rooster was crossing the intersection in front of me with the haughty self-assurance and entitlement of a pedestrian in Manhattan. He arrived at the corner alcove of a nineteenth-century stone building, which sheltered the doorway to Maya, a Mexican restaurant. The fowl paused for a moment as a trio of slender young blonde women in chic urban black entered the building. Before the door recoiled, the bird strutted in.

TO GRASP WHAT MADE SONOMA so unique in all of America at the turn of the millennium, and to understand why its townspeople formed a grassroots political movement to repel the invasion of the outsiders, it would be good to know about the old-time movie palace and the flock of peacocks on Seventh Street East and the fellow who sold giant ostrich eggs at the farmer's market. But the swiftest way to appreciate the sublime differentness of Sonoma, the way to get inside its strange culture, is through the chicken saga.

On an early Monday morning at the end of April 2000, as we

were parked in front of Sonoma's city hall, waiting for the one bus of the day that could take my girlfriend, Katharine, back to her job in San Francisco, a flock of chickens surrounded our Honda Civic. They swarmed and squawked with a frighteningly manic energy. I counted eight birds in a quick glance, but they were moving too quickly to tag mentally, and the enveloping cacophony meant there were surely many more outside my range of vision. The roosters were cockfighting as vigorously and violently as combatants in a sleazy back-alley betting contest. The hens crushed up against Katharine's side of the car and blocked her door as though they were paparazzi stalking the arrival of a movie star. Maybe they were excited to see us because it was so early in the day that there was no one else there in the Plaza, which was their permanent home. We were the only distraction and entertainment for a bunch of barnyard exiles who had adapted rather effectively to their new environment: They had become accustomed to the nearly constant stimulation of human companionship.

The scene attracted a bunch of curious ducks, who seemed restless by the pond that took up much of the Plaza's western flank. They wandered over tentatively and watched for a while before their wings exploded with fluid motion. They flew swooping loops around us, then sliced low and perilous trajectories between the chickens.

The next morning the town's newspaper, the Sonoma *Index-Tribune*, ran a bold headline that wouldn't be found in any other paper in the United States: "ROOSTER ATTACKS!"

The full story began:

ROOSTER ATTACKS BOY AT SONOMA PLAZA
CHICKENS KNOWN TO CAUSE PROBLEMS

A 3-year-old Santa Rosa boy suffered lacerations on his face and head when a rooster attacked the child during a family trip to the duck pond at Sonoma Plaza over the weekend. . . .

The boy, little Ian Austen, was looking at the comparatively dull scene of a duck sitting on eggs when suddenly he was enthused to see a rooster. He squatted and leaned over so he could study the creature nearly eye-to-eye. The bird responded with a mad flurry of violence, allegedly jumping on the boy's chest, knocking him down, climbing on his face, and clawing him viciously. His mother, Nikki, finally managed to kick the bird away. "It pierced his earlobe to the neck and just missed an eye by a quarter inch," she told the reporter. A city worker witnessed the attack and responded as though it were a killing spree, calling the police, firefighters, and paramedics. "The police officer told me what a sore spot this is politically, but that you just can't do anything about it," said the Good Samaritan. "Apparently this is not the first time, but it is the most severe."

As the story developed during the week and more details emerged, it turned out that roosters had made *three* separate attacks on small children over the past weekend, and mothers came forward to report two other recent assaults. What first appeared to be an isolated incident was actually a rampage.

Everyone in the town seemed to be talking about the news.

In the tasting room of the Ravenswood winery, a middle-aged woman was pouring zinfandel while she chatted with two younger male colleagues.

"You try to raise chickens for a while but you get tired of 'em and you want to get rid of 'em and then what are you gonna do?"

"You can't flush 'em down the toilet like an alligator!"

"People drop 'em off at the car wash."

"I've seen plenty of hens and roosters at the Seven-Eleven."

"People drop 'em off in the middle of the night. And then they multiply!"

"My next-door neighbor had a whole lot of chickens. We live in a condo complex and it's got tiny backyards. The condo board had to stop him. I said, 'You know, if this was zoned agricultural, I would have ducks!' The chicken guy was always running around trying to catch 'em. He owned a grocery store in town, and he liked to say, 'Where do you think my chickens come from?' "

WHEN THE TOWN'S PAPER came out again (it was published only on Tuesdays and Fridays), the chicken story made the front page. However small-time the Sonoma *Index-Tribune* might have seemed, it had an outsized pride: The paper has been run by the same family for a century, and everyone in the town read it. The broadsheet's logo was in Gothic type, as though it were the *New York Times*, and it enjoyed a similar impact, albeit within in its own modest realm.

Below the fold on page one, a color photograph portrayed a quartet of the Plaza birds: "Rustic reminder or taloned terror?" asked the caption. The reader learned that the first "assailant"—the rooster who nearly gouged the eye of the three-year-old—was still at large in the park. In the second attack, a two-year-old boy chased after a bunch of chickens until one retaliated by scratching him and pecking above his lip. In the third incident, another child was "severely scratched."

The reporter was covering the story with a certain restraint, at least within the careful confines of page one, but when the text jumped inside the paper to a continuation on page ten, it began to seem like some kind of joke. A police report about one of the previous month's attacks quoted a mother as saying: "A cock came close to my daughter," as if the charge were sexual harassment. The reader's gullibility was tested further by this paragraph: "Bob Cannard, a former City Councilmen who has long raised chickens in his backyard, said yesterday that the problem is simple: too many roosters and not enough hens, which makes the male birds more aggressive."

Sexually frustrated roosters?

Was it plausible that the supposed expert on poultry had a surname that was the French word for "duck"? It sounded suspicious, especially since the slang meaning of "canard" (properly spelled with only one "n") is "a fake or a hoax." Was the double entendre a tip-off that the story was a satire?

Apparently not. There was a murmured but agitated debate among the chicken lovers at the Basque Boulangerie Café, where the locals congregated in the mornings. It was as though they were parents whose teenage sons were arrested for bar brawling. Some were embarrassed, while others took an unapologetic attitude of "boys will be boys." And one old-timer even had the brazenness to blame the victims. "Those children had to be from the city," he said. "A Sonoma child would know how to handle himself around a chicken."

THE FOLLOWING WEEK the chickens made the front page of the countywide daily newspaper, the Santa Rosa *Press-Democrat*. The space above the fold was nearly filled with action-filled color photos of a trio of Sonoma's city workers frantically chasing a "rogue rooster" in and out of the bushes until one of the pursuers grabbed the bird by the neck and removed it from the park.

"SNARED IN SONOMA," said the headline. The story described how the plaintive mothers of lacerated children wanted the entire flock removed, not just the two or three roosters that eyewitnesses identified as culprits of the crimes. In response, the paper quoted a "local businessman" named Jerry Marino as an outspoken defender of the chickens: "It is unique and it is Sonoma," he said. "There aren't too many places where a semi truck will stop to let the chickens cross the road. They're beautiful birds and I hope they're here to stay."

The reporter somehow neglected to mention that Mr. Marino was the owner of the Chicken Car Wash, an open-air twenty-four-hour self-service place where teenage boys came after midnight to hose down their girlfriends' T-shirts while ostensibly cleaning their autos. The car wash was left unattended by humans most of the time, but it was watched over continually by its own flock of chickens living on the asphalt premises and in the weedy abandoned lot right next to it, where they strutted around with total freedom. They subsisted happily on scraps of leftover decaying junk-food from customers' cars.

Everyone at the Basque Café was talking about the chicken attacks. A few people turned to an old-timer, asking what he knew about "the meeting."

"There's a meetin' today," he said as he sat at the counter, visibly cheerful to have hot information, "about the roosters! That mother is making a big problem. The city council is gonna have a special meetin' this afternoon."

"If one teenager is a problem, you don't get rid of all the teenagers," said one of the other seniors. "It should be the same thing with the roosters. You know, I used to have a chicken. When I was in the Kiwanis, the club over in Petaluma gave us a chicken. I kept it in my yard. Caught it with a long steel rod."

THE NEXT AFTERNOON I was overcome with surprise and anger. On the front page of the *Press-Democrat*, above the fold, the headline read:

SONOMA BANISHES PLAZA CHICKENS

The City Council voted unanimously Wednesday night to remove all chickens from Sonoma Plaza after hearing from parents of children bloodied by rowdy roosters during the past week. The council decided public safety outweighs the rural charm that the wandering chickens lend to the plaza.

I stared at the text, incredulous. How could they do this? It only took a week of living in Sonoma to realize that the chickens were the symbol of the town's uniqueness. They represented its irreverence and most of all its anachronisms, its defiant refusal to accept the inevitability of modern life.

I tore through the paper to get to the story's continuation on the inside. Buried near the end of the text, the reporter offered a reason for hope. The mayor said that the chickens could return if the town came up with a safety plan. They would talk about the possibilities when the council met again in two weeks.

And then I wondered: Have they already taken away the chickens, perhaps never to return? Were all the birds chased and captured?

I hurried to the Plaza and ran past the rose garden and the fountains until I could spot a lone chicken strutting in front of city hall. At least there was one. And then, by the duck pond, I saw the rest of the flock. I knew it was silly to try to count the moving targets, but I counted—five, six, seven, eight. And at fifteen I finally sat down, exhausted by my anxiety and affection for this bizarre place.

THE CHICKENS, I was happy to learn, were not without defenders. I had not arrived in Sonoma just in time to see its marks of individuality taken away. Tom Whitworth, for one, would not allow that to happen. Sonoma had saved his life and he was determined to return the favor.

Whitworth was in his late fifties and looked professorial with his salt-and-pepper beard. He was a creative intellectual but he had a subversive, mischievous, passionate, combative nature rather than a cool, scholarly detachment. He had grown up in a working-class family in the industrial north of England. Through his shrewdness, energy, and abundant chutzpah, he had achieved an unlikely success as a marketing and advertising executive at big-name companies in London and later San Francisco. At one point he earned a considerable amount of money and lived in Pacific Heights, the most fashionable and exclusive neighborhood in the bay city, where he lived as an unrepentant bon vivant.

His life had changed utterly when he crashed his motorcycle and nearly died. Afterward he left the business realm, came to Sonoma, and went bohemian. He wanted to develop his talents as an artist and to live in closer appreciation of the natural world. He moved into an old barn that the owner, himself a sculptor whose large metalworks littered the yard, had partitioned into a row of inexpensive lofts. Tom learned to draw, and he completed art projects about the environment for museums and parks. He made more rent money by driving to San Francisco one day a week to roast beans for a coffeehouse. His neighbors in Sonoma included Pete, an unreformed old long-haired hippie whose friends came by to set up a tepee and take peyote and bang drums all night in Native American sweat rituals, and a man I'll call Harry, a retired bureaucrat whose friends, a bunch of six-foot-tall men with broad shoulders and hairy legs wearing gowns and high heels, came by for cross-dressing parties. Another neighbor fed bagels to his geese. A flock of wild peacocks lived in the neighborhood and made weirdly eerie, plaintive cries.

I first encountered Tom at the city council chambers. I arrived at six-thirty, a half-hour before the meeting was scheduled to begin, just to make sure that I would get a seat. The setting looked like a large courtroom, with an elevated dais for the five council members and a low wooden divider protecting them from the gallery of spectators. Already the rows were filled with angry citizens. A little girl with blonde pigtails wore a denim jacket with cartoon characters covering her back. She held a plastic model of a chicken in a wicker basket on her lap. This was the same child who showed up at the last council meeting with a live chicken in her basket; city officials had forced her to take her pet out of the building. Her father claimed that the stunt was meant to show that small children can handle chickens very safely. She was a political activist while still in elementary school.

The meeting began and the mayor opened the floor to the restless public.

"Everyone but a few fearful mothers and city council members knows the chickens are a good thing for Sonoma," said an elderly white-haired man, reading slowly from a prepared text. "When the traffic stops for chickens, it's a good thing for our humanity. In winter, it gives courage to hear the triumphant crowing of the roosters. The solution is simple if we turn to our rural Sonoma instincts: Send back the excess roosters, or have more hens to keep them docile."

"These chickens have been in this town probably since General Vallejo," said a thirtyish man. (Mariano Vallejo was the Mexican general who had owned most of Sonoma in the early nineteenth century.)

"I was raised on a farm and I know that chickens aren't just good for barbecue," he said. "Chickens eat a lot of bugs. I've seen 'em run off snakes."

"Seeing the chickens was one of the most beautiful things I've ever experienced," said a woman who worked in one of the stores in the Plaza.

Tom Whitworth approached the podium, wearing a tweedy gray blazer. He displayed a large placard with a bold-faced bulleted outline of his main points, as though he was making a marketing presentation to a corporate board. He spoke with an English accent, an actor's flair, and the outraged zeal of a political activist.

"We will hold rallies!" he said. "We will sign petitions! We will put a referendum on the ballot! We'll set up a nonprofit with media mailings and flyers and e-mail spam and a website. We'll hold a Chicken Day and chicken shows and a crowing contest. We'll hold a charity fund-raiser. I venture to say that the only place there won't be chickens this time next year will be on the city council!"

The battle had begun.

BOB CANNARD, SR., was a chicken historian as well as a chicken farmer. After three weeks of refusing to believe in his existence whenever the newspaper would quote his overly perfect double entendre of a surname, I finally met him at the city council meeting. At seventy-five he looked like an aging Wild West cowboy.

He had a bushy white mustache and black-and-white hair that was growing longish in the back. He was a gadfly, a broadly comical figure, but the locals treated him with considerable respect because of his knowledge, his age, and his forty years of passionate involvement in the life and the affairs of the town.

"You need a managed flock," he told the council members authoritatively. "The chickens can be as well managed as the flowers in the Plaza. There's more of a chance of being injured if somebody falls on a rose bush!"

He must have made an impression, because the mayor said that he would meet with Bob to talk about principles of chicken management.

On a Friday morning I went to visit Bob and his birds.

Walking across the Plaza at around ten o'clock, I noticed a chic slender blonde woman parking a silver Porsche Boxter and a clone of the woman emerging from a red Ferrari. The vanguard of rich outsiders was arriving earlier and earlier for their weekend getaways now that it was late May and Sonoma's daytime temperatures were reaching the eighties.

Bob's redwood barn was at the northern edge of the town, where he could look directly across the open grassy plain of the state park to General Vallejo's house and the hills. The coops held many chickens and a few wild turkeys, which he would soon set free into the Mayacamas. He had already nurtured a whole flock of turkeys and released them into the hillsides.

We sat together amid the clutter of scattered building materials and old machinery outside the barn's entrance.

"A couple of the city council members are *stupid*," he said. "The sixty-person staff at city hall can't understand how to manage chickens on the Plaza, which any fifteen-year-old boy used to be able to do."

When I asked why the chickens seem so vitally important to the collective psyche of this place, he responded with a brief but enlightening history lesson.

Sonoma was ruled for centuries by the native tribes, he said, and then for a short time by the Spanish colonialists, and then by the Mexicans, and then by the American military. But just about anyone with ambition left the valley to take part in the Gold Rush in the 1850s, and Sonoma fell into a half-century of stagnation. The only stimulant that interrupted the long sluggishness came when hustlers promoted the hot springs outside the town as health resorts with "salubrious" waters. Actually, the place smelled awful, but city folks came anyway. The health spas soaked up so much water that they lowered the valley's water table, draining five thousand acres of wetlands and turning Sonoma's swamps into a very promising spot for farming. The only thing they needed was farmers. A small number of peasants who emigrated from southern Europe, mostly Italy, settled there. But the biggest migration was inspired by the great earthquake and fire that devastated San Francisco in 1906. Many city dwellers, distraught and homeless, realized that they could make a viable living as poultry farmers on a mere ten acres in the country, and the ventures wouldn't take much capital. The humble chicken revived Sonoma's economy for the twentieth century. And many of today's Sonomans had grandparents or great-grandparents who settled here because of the chickens. The chicken was the valley's great savior. And now the Plaza's chickens, the symbols of the town, were banished.

"We have lost a connection to our roots," Bob Cannard said.

He grimaced.

"These people today don't have any gumption," he added.

When I came back to his barn a few days later, he said that he had met with the mayor and the city manager and given them three suggestions.

First, he called for the return of all the hens with one capon (a.k.a., castrated rooster) for every six hens. The neutered birds wouldn't be driven to sublimate their frustrated sexual aggression by responding with violence to the taunts of rambunctious school-children.

Second, he recommended that the chickens should be fitted with identification bands, so workers could tell the officially sanctioned city chickens from the orphans that irresponsible people dropped off at midnight and that might include sexually active cocks.

Third, he envisioned a "Sonoma Chicken Patrol" that would hand out informational leaflets and try to educate the people on the Plaza about how to act in the presence of poultry.

He said that if they adopted this plan, then once again "the citizens of Sonoma can enjoy the slower pace of life that the chickens require of us all."

ON A WEDNESDAY NIGHT in early June, as the meeting to reconsider the fate of the chickens was about to begin, Bob Cannard arrived at the city council chamber. He wore beige plaid pants and a shirt with a cowboy-style tie beneath a bathrobe—a bathrobe!—so remarkably colorful that it was nearly psychedelic.

"I didn't want to wear a sports jacket, so I wore my bathrobe," he said.

He also wore a black hat with a brim. The overall effect made him look even more like an old gunfighter, with the bathrobe like a long cowhide coat.

As he entered the chambers, the gallery was filled with angry citizens who were hoping that tonight their elected officials would finally listen to their will.

The city manager reported that Mr. Cannard, a noted local authority on poultry, had recommended Mediterranean chicken species for the Plaza.

"Mediterranean breeds or hybrids are best because they can fly and get away from children," she said.

The mayor opened the floor to the public.

An old Italian-American woman approached the microphone.

"My mamma taught her children common sense," she said.

"But today these dot-com mammas, they no teach their children any common sense!" When she said "dot-com mammas," her voice had a bitingly satirical contempt. "These dot-com mammas think they're so good. They not as good as my mamma!"

The audience erupted with approving laughter.

After a few more speakers who were nearly as openly hostile, the mayor finally succeeded in ending the public discussion. He asked the council members to elucidate their own positions and then cast their votes.

Al Mazza voted yes to returning the chickens. He wanted to try out Bob Cannard's proposals for six months.

Louis Ramponi voted no.

"My parents raised chickens, sold eggs, sold chickens for barbecues," he said. "Chickens to me are a food source. They'll never be pets. They're a wild animal. That's my decision because that's the way I was raised."

Ken Brown, an ally of Tom Whitworth and the voice of Sonoma's bohemian element, voted yes.

The chicken fans were ahead two-to-one.

But then Phyllis Carter voted no. Even though the city manager had explained that Sonoma's insurance covered rooster attacks, she was still concerned about the liability issues.

"It's just like a dog off a leash," she said.

She was also worried about protecting the chickens from being attacked or injured by the town's rambunctious children.

"This is not Disneyland!" she exclaimed. "These are *animals*!"

With the score tied at two–two, the deciding vote belonged to the current mayor, Larry Barnett. With his bulky torso and his well-pressed dress shirt and his conservative necktie and the spectacular redness of his plump cheeks, he looked like a caricature of a prosperous small-town banker from a bygone era. Actually he was an epitome of an earlier wave of urban refugees who went native in bohemian Sonoma, a man who was living the dream. He used to be the cofounder and top executive of a publicly traded company in the Silicon Valley region, but now he owned a charming Victorian bed-and-breakfast, the Thistle Dew Inn, while he also ran a small web page design practice. In his public appearances he was an outspoken critic of the increasing dominance of giant global corporations in the world economy. And he was an impassioned advocate of grassroots political involvement and the virtues of community and direct democracy. With the wellspring of public support for returning the chickens, there was no surprise when Larry finally announced his vote:

"Yes."

The chickens had won three-to-two. They were coming back.

The audience left the room, feeling elated and vindicated.

Outside, the people crowded around their savior, Bob Cannard.

"They couldn't vote against you Bob," one of his fans said. "You look like Wyatt Earp!"

I ARRIVED as an outsider in Sonoma, though with my sympathies quickly engaged by the chicken debate, I was determined to go native. But Sonoma was getting only too used to outsiders, and I must have looked like just another one of the invaders.

Sonoma had several guises. Much as "New York" could mean either the borough of Manhattan, or the greater city of five boroughs, or the larger state, "Sonoma" could mean four things: the town, the valley, the mountain, or the county. The town of Sonoma was the largest of the three small towns in the Sonoma Valley, which lay directly west of the Napa Valley, separated by the Mayacamas Mountains. To get between the two valleys, you had to drive over the top of the Mayacamas, climbing twenty-eight hundred feet and then descending, or around them through the wetlands at the north of the bay. The Sonoma Valley was bordered on its east by the Mayacamas and on its west by Sonoma Mountain. And beyond Sonoma Mountain was the rest of Sonoma County, which had a half-dozen other wine-producing valleys and a long stretch of Pacific coastline.

The invasion's target was specifically Sonoma the town and the valley, which were the closest to Napa on the map and also looked the most like it. The two valleys were like country cousins in many ways. Their histories, from the 1860s to the 1960s, were remarkably similar. Sonoma followed the same narrative of a flourishing wine trade eviscerated by phylloxera and Prohibition, leaving country hamlets that were bypassed by the new freeways and seemingly lost in a sleepy time warp. But the destinies of the two valleys began to diverge in the sixties and seventies. While Napa was transformed from a provincial backwater into a bastion of luxury and status, Sonoma became a refuge for free-spirited counterculture types from the California cities. Mario Savio, the charismatic leader of the student revolt at Berkeley in the sixties, settled in as a professor at Sonoma State. The local community college became a mecca for hippies who wanted to learn about organic farming so they could go "back to the land." Sonoma turned into a new bohemia, a place where iconoclasts, eccentrics, and activists could live the good life on the cheap. Artists converted old barns into loft spaces for homes and studios. Aging hippies found farmland where they could put up tepees and take peyote and bang drums through the night in Native American sweat-lodge rituals. Buddhists and poets and ecstatic dance teachers all found an amenable home. By the end of the nineties, Sonoma was a lot like Berkeley in the country.

Through it all the bohemians lived harmoniously with the other types who had been there before they arrived: the shitkicker farmers and the unsophisticated small-town natives. There were plenty of wine people, too, and Sonoma was second only to Napa in the *Wine Spectator* surveys of their readers' interest in American wines, though it was a distant second, trailing twenty-one percent to seventy percent. But Sonoma's grape growers and winemakers didn't aspire to Napa's image of elegance and refinement. They reacted against Napa's pretentiousness and promoted themselves as offbeat, down-home, and quirky, much in the spirit of the bohemians and the shitkickers they lived among. While Napa was Robert Mondavi in black tie, the best-known personalities among the Sonoma vintners were seventies pop-culture holdovers such as Tommy Smothers, the comedian famous for playing with yo-yos on television, and Bruce Cohn, the manager of the Doobie Brothers band.

It was more frustrating for rich outsiders to build in Sonoma than Napa. "Sonoma is *harder*," Olle Lundberg, a prominent modernist architect in San Francisco who built twenty villas in Napa for wealthy clients in the nineties, complained. "The planning department is much more obstructionist. They have an 'insider' attitude. If you don't have an office there . . ." he rolled his eyes. "They're very much trying to prevent growth."

Many of the new-money invaders liked how Sonoma hadn't been overrun by more of their kind the way that Napa had. While some of the *new* new-money people wanted into the *old* new-money club in the Napa Valley, this different breed of new new money wanted the appearance of old old money. They liked how Sonoma felt more authentically "country" than Napa in the same way that Vermont and northwestern Connecticut seemed more sui generis than the Hamptons, with their transplanted Manhattan social scenes. And Sonoma was strangely reminiscent of many of the provincial places where the new-money people had grown up. Sonoma evoked in them an unexpectedly powerful nostalgia for the backwaters they had struggled so hard to get out of.

"Sonoma is very *Southern*," my friend Celia Canfield told me approvingly as we sat in a Starbucks in her affluent neighborhood in San Francisco. She drawled it out unironically as "Suuuuh-thun." She still got away with playing the belle even though she had left Alabama nearly twenty years earlier, studied at Oxford, lived in Cairo, then earned her windfall as a senior executive at a techno-media empire in Silicon Valley, and though her clothes were black and Italian for our casual afternoon rendezvous at a neighborhood café. Her girlish slenderness, healthy straight brown hair, and fair skin gave her an air of youthful vitality at forty-one, as did having a handsome boyfriend, David Applebaum, who was six years her junior. He had worked at Oracle and now he was an executive at a software startup. Together they had bought a perfect little weekend house in the town of Sonoma.

And they were offering me the key.

"The wine country reminds me of the South," Celia said. "The world moves more slowly up there. It's *agrarian*," she said, intoning the word with gentle reverence.

"Most of the new money is going to the Napa side. It's more Disneylike in Napa. There isn't the sense of community that we have in Sonoma. Sonoma is the *old* wine country. Napa is new. It's a tourist place contrived by the wineries. There's a real Sonoma–Napa split. Sonoma is like Alabama and Mississippi. Napa is like Florida." Meaning that Sonoma was real country, admirably anti-quated, while Napa was an ersatz place blighted by urban arrivistes (not the benign kind like Celia and David, of course, but the truly egregious kind).

Celia and David probably paid thirty or forty times as much for their weekend cottage as their native Sonoma neighbors had spent, however many years ago, for their *only* homes. But these newcom-ers wanted fervently to be seen as locals, not as antisocial "weekend people" antipathetic to the besieged natives. They craved the con-cept of community. They yearned to fit in and become accepted there. To be *insiders*. They strived to immerse themselves in the vil-lage's life. The Plaza hosted outdoor festivals or parades on most summer weekends, and Celia and David could be seen at every one. But no matter how diligently and visibly they participated in the town's events, Celia knew that the other people on their block persisted in referring to them, with suspicion and distrust, as "the outsiders."

"Still, it's delightful to be up there," Celia said that afternoon in the city, "because none of the neighbors understand the technology business or care about it at all." She added: "They really don't have any idea what we do," and she smiled with conspiratorial bemusement, as if she were describing the culture of an aboriginal tribe that had eluded the corrupting influences of civilization.

IF CELIA AND DAVID were unlikely to give me entrance to the "real" Sonoma, it was outright laughable to think that my other Sonoma connection, Ann Winblad, could play that part. While Celia and David personified the spirit of the millionaires migrating to Sonoma, Ann Winblad was a good proxy for the centimillionaires going there. She was famous as a software entrepreneur and venture capitalist and appeared frequently on television and in the national press.

We had met in 1992 when I was writing a *Fortune* cover story about Bill Gates. Ann, who lived in San Francisco, had maintained a long-distance romance with Bill, in Seattle, for four years in the eighties, and she remained one of his closest confidantes. Ann and I realized that we were neighbors in Pacific Heights, even though I rented a one-bedroom apartment in an ugly concrete high-rise apartment building off on the edges and she owned a lovely free-standing four-story Edwardian house at the heart of the neighborhood. Occasionally I would walk over and we'd order in pizza and watch old movies on the projection screen in her attic, which she had had rebuilt into a TV room. And several times she had me over on weekends to her wooded ten-acre estate in Glen Ellen, a hamlet in the western foothills of the Sonoma Valley.

Ann grew up in the boondocks of Minnesota, where her father was a high school football coach, and she liked how Glen Ellen felt like a small town in middle America.

At the same time, the actual neighbors irritated her. When she went to the grocery store, she would pretend not to see any of the several top executives from Intel who lived in the vicinity and might want to talk about business.

The natives were a bigger problem. The artists from the cottage down the road had a habit of swimming in Ann's pool and playing on her tennis court when she wasn't there, as if it were communal property. And the bumpkins across the street had permanently dumped the contents of their garages out onto their yards, scattering around all kinds of broken-down pieces of junk.

Ann was a longtime friend of mine and a generous host, and when I mentioned that I wanted to spend my weekdays in the Sonoma Valley, she didn't hesitate to offer me her keys. But she did ask for something in return:

"Your job is to spy on my neighbors," she said. "Find out what it will take for me to buy their properties."

FOR ALL OF ITS anachronistic charm and its many other virtues, and despite all my enthusiasm, I soon realized that Sonoma wasn't the perfect town that it might seem to be on a casual visit. Much like the Napa Valley, it was surprisingly segregated by class. In Napa they asked whether you lived "up valley" or "down valley," and then they thought they knew all about you. In the town of Sonoma, you might try to get away with saying that your home was on Second Street or Fifth Street, but they would ask "east or west," and then your socioeconomic profile would most likely have been revealed.

The east side was the classier side. The west side was more middle or working class. Its landscaping wasn't as lush and many of its residences weren't kept up so caringly. While the east side had only houses, the west side had low-rise apartments and mobile-home parks as well, and its residential sections were interlaced with noise and traffic from strip malls and supermarkets.

Beyond the working-class haven of the west side came the Springs, which were once known for their natural hot-springs resorts for day-tripping city folks. Long ago the waters dried up and the area became a refuge of the lower classes: Mexican farmhands and homegrown white trash. The Springs also attracted a cohort of liberal political activists and artists and other class-diving bohemians, who lived in the dense woods behind a ratty strip of taco joints and bodegas.

In explaining the geography, Celia Canfield recalled the Deep South of her childhood: "The east side and west side of Sonoma are like east Tennessee versus west Tennessee," she said. Tennessee's western flats had the wealth of the cities, while its eastern reaches harbored the lingering poverty and backwardness of the Appalachian hills. But that was the old South, and this was turn-of-the-century *California*. How unbelievable that it could be so segregated and hierarchical, just like a rural town in the 1950s.

Sonoma's east side, where Celia and David had their cottage, rivaled Napa's exclusive St. Helena for loveliness. The architecture had an appealingly modest, human scale. Many of the houses had just one story, and they were noticeably small by today's bloated standards of moneyed display. They were bungalows and cottages, not mansions and fortresses and villas. There were some graceful Victorians from the second half of the nineteenth century but they were outnumbered by the Arts and Crafts creations from the first half of the twentieth. There was a mix of restrained postwar good neighbors, mostly shingled or barn-sided wooden houses, and a few Mediterranean-style ones, but nothing modern or shocking. The lots, like the houses, were small. The most impressive thing about the east side was the profusion of flowers, particularly the roses by the white picket fences and the bougainvillea covering the arched trellises. The landscaping made even the most humble cottages seem attractive. In places there were high, thick palm trees and an abundance of cacti and other succulents, which added a bit of exoticism and a western feel. Californians liked to compare Sonoma and Napa with the fabled rural regions of Europe, but you weren't likely to find a cactus anywhere in Provence or Tuscany.

The east side was reminiscent of other old California towns, especially Berkeley. In both places the lushly abundant landscap-

ing overwhelmed the Craftsman cottages. But Berkeley was different because it was wildly overgrown, as if nature couldn't restrain
its exuberance there. Sonoma had a similar natural beauty but it
seemed better groomed and more conscientiously cared for.

The east side's compactness enhanced the strong feeling of
neighborhood. Broadway marked the center of town and divided
the east and west sides. Celia's house was on Fifth Street East, the
last street inside city limits, only five blocks from the center. Not
far beyond, the town turned into the country, the character became
rural, and the lots consisted of expansive acreages. A Sonoman
didn't need a car. Anyone could easily walk from their own home
to the Plaza or, with a little more exertion, to anyplace else in the
village. The terrain was utterly flat, and a casual bicyclist could
cover it in only a few minutes. Sonoma was small enough for the
old-fashioned notion of community to exist still.

There was one stretch that marred the harmonious character of
the east side. On the far side of Fifth Street, there was an enclave
that looked like it must have been the nearest farm on the outskirts
of the old village. At the center of this property stood an exceptionally proud, elegant, and well-maintained house, a house that
was really a mansion, with covered walkways leading through
tended lawns to outbuildings as large as many Sonoma cottages. It
was obvious from the transplanted newness of the surrounding trees
that not too long ago the rest of the large acreage had been the
cleared-off farm terrain. But now the mansion was ringed by about
two dozen subdivided lots, about half of which had sprouted huge
multimillion-dollar houses, conspicuously and gratingly new. They
were far too shiny, even though they tried to be good citizens by
aping the historical styles from the town. Most of the houses were
overblown Victorian fantasies. A few imitated the Craftsman look
but without the modest scale that was part of the movement's ex-
plicit philosophy. The houses were probably four or five times as
large as their village counterparts, so sprawling that they appeared
uncomfortably cramped in their relatively tight lots. They seemed

much more expensively built than the ubiquitous copycat McMansions, cheaply made tract houses on steroids, proliferating in suburbs across the nation. McMansions are the residential equivalent of greasy fast-food burger meals gone "supersize." Instead of spending more money for fresher and leaner and more nutritious cuisine, the "supersize" customer wants not one but two of the same tasteless meat patties; the same fatty fries, just twice as much; the same sugary drink, twice as big. The McMansion buyer got the same cheap construction, with bigger rooms.

These homes, in contrast, had some exquisite architectural details, but too many of them. It was like a chef who discovered the ingredients of classic French cuisine and then couldn't restrain himself from lumping foie gras, black truffles, crème fraiche, and caviar all in the same dish rather than picking one luxurious touch to stand out. The scale of these houses was simply arrogant. The covered porches alone had more square footage than a nice bungalow. The lawns were fiercely exhibitionistic. The flora was gorgeous. But while the village's flowers wandered in all directions with natural exuberance, these were arranged neatly in groomed beds with a geometrical precision that revealed the heavy hand of humans. The flowers around cottages in the old town were like healthy country kids left alone to make their own fun, while these were like rich children who were carefully monitored at all times by strict nannies.

The enclave had a disturbingly ersatz quality, as if this were a lavish theme park inspired by the real thing just across the street, but redone with a size and glitz and plasticity and orderliness that ruined the illusion of reality. It was as if the builders convinced themselves and their ignorant millionaire clients that they wanted to celebrate the town, while actually hubristically thinking they could improve on it. But the worst thing about the development was the ring of ugly, weedy grass that surrounded it. These unkempt lots hadn't been sold just yet. By letting them grow wild, the developer wasn't just creating an eyesore for the people in less expensive homes across the street, but digging a symbolic moat to protect the elites of the estates from the proles of the town. The gesture was defiantly antisocial, a stupidly mean-spirited attack on the underlying notion of community, the arrivistes snubbing the old-timers.

A large sign heralded the development as "Armstrong Estates," but Celia's boyfriend David called it "the McWine houses." The developer was a Sonoma native named Steve Noble Ledson, and he lived in the old mansion at the center. Ledson's son, who had been drinking at an event at the family's winery, had driven off a road at night, killing his fiancée. The fiancée's family was suing Ledson's company. Some of the townspeople despised Ledson so much for building the Armstrong Estates and inviting in the moneyed outsiders that they were quietly rooting for the lawsuit to bring him to financial ruin.

THROUGH CELIA, I met my first genuine Sonoma locals. Brad and Sue Gross lived directly across Fifth Street East from Celia and David. The Grosses seemed to be the only locals who were close with the wealthy weekenders and gave them the acceptance they openly craved. The two couples bonded over a shared characteristic—both are comprised of a Jewish man and a gentile woman—but otherwise they had little in common. Even though Brad owned a fixer-upper on the higher-class side of town, he epitomized the regular guy from the working class. He was a former sailor and ship's captain who was currently employed as the harbor master of a marina. He had tattoos. He was a volunteer fireman in Sonoma, an important symbol of masculine bravado in a place where the hillsides ignite into dangerous blazes during the hot, dry summers. He appeared to be in his late thirties, slender and fit, with straight dark hair and a mustache that gave him something of a playful air. He was gregarious and engaging.

"I bought the biggest piece of crap on the east side," he said.

"Any one of those porches at Armstrong Estates is worth more than my house."

Brad wanted to show me the gaping disparities in Sonoma real estate, so we drove to First Street East and then, for comparison, to First Street West. The houses and lots on both roads were diminutive and unpretentious, but the ones with the fetishized east side addresses sold for twice as much as their neighbors just two short blocks away. And the real estate became much more expensive as you went deeper toward the sheltered center of the east side.

"The prices are rising because people in San Francisco in the tech business are buying weekend houses," he said. "The buyers aren't young families like us. And a lot of contractors are buying crappy old houses on spec for four hundred grand, putting two hundred into the renovation, and then selling them for nine hundred, so they made a three hundred thousand profit in almost no time." He was lucky to get his own "piece of crap" a couple of years ago for three hundred, since only a wealthy couple like Celia and David could afford the east side today.

He drove eastward out of the town and across the last two miles of the valley's floor. Then the road pierced the hillside and climbed slowly, through many switchbacks, ascending high and deep into the Mayacamas. Ultimately we surfaced in a hidden valley, no more than a half-mile long and wide.

"This is the Lovell Valley," Brad said. "Look, you can see San Francisco from here. On a clear night I like to come here and see the lights of the city."

The Lovell Valley was at the very center of the mountains, halfway between the Sonoma and Napa valleys. But the only way there was the road we took from Sonoma, which then made a big loop around the valley's periphery. The land was divided into only about twenty large parcels, which were sprouting trophy houses that rivaled or surpassed the McWine monstrosities in the town.

It was the kind of place that the overclass used to shun because it seemed so remote and isolated, but that was now appealing to a certain cadre of the new money. There was a sense that they could have erected a barricade at the valley's only entrance and lived as an elite enclave, keeping out the lower classes as well as the tax collectors.

"Not too long ago you couldn't give these lots away," Brad said. "Now they've all got multimillion-dollar houses."

Even in this milieu, one house stood out for its sheer size and its boxy banality. It was surely the most charmless residence in the area. And it was on the market for $3.5 million according to the real-estate brochures in a clear plastic container attached to the mailbox. This was the house that the actress Sharon Stone leased and lived in for weeks when she was filming a forgettable movie near the bay at an abandoned naval base, where many Sonomans used to work. The gossip was that the diva, who was single at the time, tried to pick up a guy at the farmer's market, a handsome man who had some land on the outskirts of town where he made and sold old-fashioned wooden windmills. The funny thing was that this country bumpkin honestly had no idea that she was an international movie queen.

THERE WAS A PAVED PATH for walking or bicycling across the mile-long latitude of the town, moving from east to west along the northern borderline. The path had a magnificent, clear vista of Sonoma Mountain, a great green mother with her wide arms out-stretched as if she were scooping up the entire valley like a bunch of fruits and vegetables to take to the market.

The path began by traversing a vineyard. A few steps forward and you were surrounded by several acres of Sebastiani cabernet. This was part of the same plot where General Vallejo planted the northern California wine country's first vineyard in 1825.

Vallejo was the pivotal figure of nineteenth-century Sonoma, and the Sebastianis were its prime powers in the twentieth. The clan prospered by making inexpensive jug wines that were an everyday beverage for Italian immigrants like themselves. They wound up owning much of the town. It was the patriarch,

Samuele, who built the Sebastiani Theater, the beloved movie palace on the Plaza, in 1933. He also owned the cannery that employed many of the locals through the struggles of the Depression and the Second World War.

To the right, on a little knoll just beyond the vineyard, stood the house that had been home to all four generations of the Sonoma dynasty. Samuele's daughter-in-law, Sylvia Sebastiani, still lived there, an octogenarian matriarch looking out from her picture window onto her own vineyards and winery.

The Sebastiani house was well kept and quietly charming, but surprisingly modest and rustic. The small structure had rough stone on the ground floor and a brown wood second story that covered only part of the base. It looked more like the ancestral homestead of a European peasant family lucky enough to farm a bountiful small acreage than the power center of an agribusiness dynasty that was one of the nation's largest producers of wine.

After crossing through the vineyard, the walking path headed alongside several acres of a scrappy little farm, the Patch, which was owned and run by the community as a collective and as a demonstration of organic agriculture. The plowed rows of soil were nurturing broccoli, carrots, beets, onions, and lettuces. It was a stunning setting for a farm, with the Mayacamas rising to just the north side and the green vision of Sonoma Mountain directly ahead to the west.

From the path one could see the Vella cheese factory, an old stone building that was the home to another of Sonoma's four-generation Italian dynasties. The Vellas were a Sicilian clan who handmade a cow's-milk cheese—unpasteurized, aged, and hard—that many aficionados considered the closest rival to the great parmigiano-reggiano that America ever produced.

"You have to meet the Vellas," Celia said. "Their daughters all have bizarre names, like Ditty and Chickie, as if they were characters in *Fried Green Tomatoes*."

Next the path led to a shady park where the town's original train depot stood as centerpiece, a historical remnant now that the last mile of the railroad track had been removed to make way for this walking path. The park's raison d'être was an expanse of a dozen dirt-covered courts for the traditional French pastime of *petanque*, better known in America by the name of its Italian variation, bocce. The favorite sport of European vineyard hands was an abiding passion in the American wine country as well.

The park in turn led to a cluster of Little League baseball diamonds behind a sign that honored the donors and heralded the site as the *Field of Dreams*. This was one case when the boasts of local boosters were well justified. Hollywood's dream-makers couldn't have created a better evocation of idealized life in an idyllic small town. Even they, for the sake of realism, might have added some imperfections to the crisp green grass leading to the rolling mountainside. This was exactly where you'd take a nostalgic urban father to convince him to move his family back to the country to raise his small children.

The well-tended turf of the baseball outfields gave way to a large stretch of high, burned brown grass nearly ready to be cut and bundled into hay. The land was part of a state park surrounding the historic home of General Vallejo. That two-story structure had a yellow-painted wooden shingle exterior in the European style of the nineteenth century, but beneath the wood there's a structural layer of adobe, the material that Mexicans preferred to build with. The Vallejo house, like the Sebastiani house, was small enough that it could be swallowed by any one of the bloated new McWine mansions in Amstrong Estates. Even the lord of a vast colonial land grant in a fertile valley lived in a more modest style than the newly rich of the millennium's turn.

AS I SPENT MORE TIME in Sonoma, I enthusiastically catalogued its quirks. Even the phone book was unusual. It was small (there were only nine thousand inhabitants) and it had the usual alphabetical arrangement of residents, but then there was a sneaky "reverse directory," which listed the phone numbers in ascending order. That way, if you knew just the number, you could find the name. And even if you couldn't remember the last digit or two, you could still find the person easily. I had thought that only FBI agents and police officers and investigative reporters had access to reverse directories. Everywhere else in America, the citizens were fighting to protect their privacy and anonymity, but there in Sonoma the people seemed to want every way to know their neighbors and to be known in return.

The Tuesday evening farmer's market was where the community came together. A dozen farmers parked their pickup trucks and set up tables beneath tents and awnings on the U-shaped driveway in front of city hall.

The market was a crowded scene by six o'clock. Seemingly everyone in the town came out, drawn by the socializing even more than the shopping. The pattern was that you arrived on foot or bike and even before you could pick out some arugula you came across someone you hadn't seen since last week's farmer's market and a long conversation ensued and then other friends walked by and attached themselves to the cluster. It could take two hours before you finally managed to buy a handful of vegetables in between all the schmoozing.

The farmers needed especially fine or interesting offerings if they wanted to sell produce in a town where so many people tended their own vegetable gardens or had little farms of their own. In Sonoma a resident could easily swap her black mission figs for a neighbor's beefsteak tomatoes. Or she could buy what she needed from the baskets on the porches of the cottages down the street. "You leave your money and take the produce," Brad said when we saw unattended cigar boxes and coffee canisters in front of various houses. "In this town you can leave thirty dollars in front of your yard and no one will ever steal it. And you don't need to show an ID to write a check anywhere in this town, because that's just how people are. When we first moved here, I got my car fixed and the mechanic let me take the car without paying. He just said, 'Send it to me later.' Then I went to a store that didn't take credit cards, and they told me, 'Just send a check whenever you get a chance.' They didn't even take my name or address."

Even with all the backyard gardens in Sonoma, the farmers enticed buyers with the size and variety of the produce. The selection of fresh vegetables was overwhelming. Locals filled their ecologically conscious canvas or mesh-string bags with green garlic, spring red onions, baby carrots, mesclun salad greens, asparagus, fennel, and cherries. The zucchinis and summer squash still had flowers attached. The leeks seemed unreal: as long, thick, and smooth as the light sabers from the *Star Wars* movies.

On the eastern side, near the Plaza's rose garden and its grand fountain, a plucky farmer named Shelley Arrowsmith sold eggs that her ducks had laid that morning. She also sold little cloth bags filled with fragrant French lavender, mint, hops, chamomile, and flax seed. She grew the lavender herself.

"You put this over your eyes and it helps relax you," she said.

"Are your products organic?" a customer asked.

"Yes, they are," Shelley said. "Just worm compost and chicken manure and the sparrows do a good job of eating the bugs in winter."

Shelley Arrowsmith was fortyish and wore a white tank top and shorts and had profuse freckles and long, straight red hair beneath her wide-brimmed straw hat. She had been an environmental activist in San Francisco before she left the city to work her own land. She farmed a one-acre plot herself, working and weeding even on days with 100-degree heat. The lavender and eggs were her staples, but she sometimes had fresh boysenberries she picked herself. She compensated for the limitations of her diminutive acreage and her one-woman operation by growing things that the larger farmers didn't sell at the market.

A few feet away from Shelley's pickup truck, a clutch of teenagers congregated beneath the tree-sheltered walkway. A purple-haired girl in a black leather top, metallic miniskirt, and torn black fishnet stockings taught a boy in a T-shirt how to swing dance using steps that were popular in the thirties.

Mike and Allison O'Donnell, a young couple from the east side, sold their own brand of olive oil. They leased the olive trees from one of the old vineyards. Mike, in jeans and a polo, was a fourth-generation Sonoman whose great-grandfather had come to Sonoma in 1886. He was a regular guy who couldn't seem to repress his broad grin. He looked as though he was well aware that he had married the prettiest girl in his hometown. Allison was a natural beauty with a shy and disarming smile and hypnotic blue eyes. There was a Grace Kelly quality to her as a yellow summer dress accentuated her natural blondness and her gentle tan. They looked like a Hollywood casting director's idealized vision of a rural small-town couple.

On the park's western side, in front of the pond where the flying ducks and the pecking chickens spent most of their time, there was the Ostrich Guy, an older white-bearded man in a white T-shirt and a hat with ostrich feathers. He sold frozen cuts of ostrich meat from his free-range ranch.

"Ostrich has hardly any fat," he proselytized. "It's much leaner than beef, and we don't use chemicals or growth hormones."

He also sold fresh ostrich eggs for twelve dollars each. The eggs were the size of footballs. They looked as though they were laid by dinosaurs.

There were two ways to cook an ostrich egg, the farmer said. You could hard-boil it, which took about three or four hours given its size, or you could panfry it up in a scramble or omelet and that way it cooked about as quickly as the usual diminutive chicken eggs. The catch was that one ostrich egg equaled something like four dozen chicken eggs, so you needed to invite the entire neighborhood over for brunch or you had to eat eggs every meal for three days.

The farmer's recipe called for two pieces of equipment that weren't usually associated with fine cuisine: a flashlight and a hammer.

"Sonoma Knolls Ranch," read the slip of white paper that came with the egg. "Instructions for egg extraction. Find the air space with a flashlight in a dark room. Gently tap the top until you have a hole the size of a nickel."

I tried this recipe once, but when I gave the gentle tap, nothing happened. The outer shell of the egg was too hard. I wondered what Julia Child would do. I channeled my Inner Julia and that inspired me to try greater force. I had to pound as if I was driving a large nail into a two-by-four.

The trick was to make the hole large enough to pour from but small enough not to mar the smooth elliptical form of the eggshell, which people saved as mementos. For twelve bucks, you don't throw away the shell. The farmer suggested painting it and preserving it as a sculptural objet d'art.

Not surprisingly, there were few customers for the eggs, so the farmer resorted to barbecuing ostrich burgers, which looked identical to hamburgers and had an appealingly meaty flavor without nearly as much fattiness or greasiness as ground beef. The Ostrich Guy had the fierce belief of a religious evangelist about the superiority of the ostrich as a healthy source of hormone-free lean protein. But the ostrich burgers also attracted few customers. So he finally condescended to cook cow burgers as well, and those were remarkably popular. But Ostrich Guy seemed resentful of their rapid sales and visibly guilty about his newfound success. Every time a Sonoman stepped up and ordered a beef burger rather than an ostrich one, the Ostrich Guy scowled and growled.

During the farmer's market a couple of aging hippie musicians played beneath the tall slender palm tree on the lawn that ran through the Plaza from the front of city hall to Broadway. Their tunes were in the style of the Grateful Dead: folksy, mellow, and mildly psychedelic. Young parents spread blankets on the neat grass, reaching into their wicker baskets for local wines and cheeses while their small children ran in circles or danced maniacally. Looking south, down the long vista of Broadway, you could see the brown mountains in the far distance. Looking east, west, or north, the town was surrounded by green hills.

The farmer's market was an insider's event. There weren't any of the suspicious "weekend people" there, unless you counted me, and the locals liked it that way. This was their own party, their private celebration of their town, their weekly forum for gossip and camaraderie. By holding the event on Tuesdays, from five until dusk, they virtually guaranteed that outsiders remained on the outside. A San Francisco technology millionaire might arrive on Thursday to get a head start on the weekend, or even occasionally on a Wednesday night, but never on Tuesday. A Silicon Valley mogul might stay over in town for a Monday that was a legal holiday, taking a three-day weekend, but by Tuesday he'd be back at work in Palo Alto. Even Celia, with her gastronomic passions and her cravings to be an insider, hadn't experienced this scene. "I've never been to the farmer's market," she told me at the café in the city, "but I hear that it's *fabulous*." And so it was.

THE SEBASTIANI THEATER was across the street from the Plaza. The movie palace had one of those long old-fashioned entrance arcades, open but sheltered, that led from the neon marquee on the street to the front doors of the auditorium. It was more than just a covered spot where you could stand to wait for your date or to find shelter from the rain. It was a wonderful architectural feature, creating a sense of dramatic anticipation about going from the public space of the street to the inner sanctuary of the cinema, a special place apart from the world.

At the front of the arcade there was a freestanding glass-enclosed ticket-seller's window. I walked up to pay for my admission to the movie, but it turned out that the woman sitting behind the glass was actually a realistic life-sized mannequin dressed in vintage clothing. A ribbon pinned to her white cardigan sweater identified her as "Miss Personality 1941."

Miss Personality wore a boxy greenish hat and thick black-framed eyeglasses with sleek catwoman curves—the kind of eye-wear that was back in style with young urban hipsters after a half-century hiatus. The kids on Haight Street in the city would have loved these frames. Miss P. also sported a flower-shaped pin on her demure woolen sweater. She sat in front of an old-time tele-phone with a rotary dial at its base and a tube to speak into at the top. Apparently the latest phone call had taken her away from the game of Autobridge on her lap. Autobridge was a mechanized single-player version of the popular four-handed game of bridge, a lost era's equivalent of an electronic game. She was surrounded by well-preserved accoutrements and forgotten drugstore items from the thirties, forties, and fifties, which rested on the inside ledge of her booth: aspirin tablets (49 cents for two bottles of 100), cold creams, hair oils, face powders, cake makeup, antacid powders. The brand names and the packagings would evoke nostalgia for my mother and my grandmothers. Miss Personality also had two bottles of mineral water from the Springs, which got to the "designer wa-ter" trend a few decades ahead of Calistoga in the Napa Valley. But its springs ran dry long before the trend became a national obsession.

The theater's owner, Roger Rhoten, was standing by the inner doors, selling the tickets himself. As the line moved forward, Roger appeared to know every customer. He greeted them all by name and took a prolonged moment to chat with each individual and catch up on their news while the rest of the people waited with an easy patience that would confound a city dweller. When it was my turn, I took out a ten-dollar bill, expecting to receive just quarters in return, but the admission to the first-run feature was only $3.50, astonishingly cheap, as though Sonoma really were stuck back in the era of Miss Personality.

Roger was also a professional magician. On certain weekend

nights, or whenever he felt inspired, he performed his magic act as a prelude to the film. Some nights he engaged an old-time crooner to sing a few numbers for the crowd. Tonight he seemed too busy selling tickets, and the film began without a lead-in.

The feature was *High Fidelity*, starring John Cusack as a single guy looking for sex and love in bohemian Chicago. I had already seen the film in San Francisco, but I wanted to watch how the Sonoma audience reacted to it. Compared to the city cineastes, the small-town crowd laughed twice as loudly at the exchanges of racy dialogue and the protagonist's ironic riffs.

The moviegoers here weren't as jaded and world-weary. Sonomans still thought that R-rated flicks were sexy and a bit scandalous.

THE LACK OF A STARBUCKS also marked Sonoma as somewhat outside the American mainstream. The national gourmet coffee chains hadn't come to Sonoma, and they weren't wanted. Instead of Starbucks Sonoma had a beloved homegrown establishment, the Basque Boulangerie Café across from the Plaza on First Street East. The locals referred to it as the Basque or, if they were trying to show off their chumminess with the owner, as Francoise's. Every morning the small storefront was a vibrant scene. It would be hard to overstate how happy everyone seemed. The men wore baseball hats with logos from Goodyear or other agricultural-industrial firms. This wasn't the place to show off the insignias of Ralph Lauren or Calvin Klein.

The customers ordered huge pastries. The choice at the glass-covered display was overwhelming: strudels, danishes, brioches, butterhorns, croissants, turnovers, elephant ears, bear claws, muffins, rolls, breads, cookies. The patrons sat down at the half-dozen tables or along the U-shaped wine bar, a speckled counter that looked like it belonged in a luncheonette from a lost era. It was surrounded by swivel seats anchored to the floor by tall metal cylinders, like the kind that used to hold up the chairs in old barbershops.

The locals slathered plenty of butter on their heroic pastries. Sometimes, amazingly, a Sonoman would consume two of the oversized creations. It was a pronounced difference from the San Francisco cafés where the habitués worried about mistaking the two-percent milk for the skim milk and pouring a few drops of fat into their cups. The Basque didn't have any skim milk. It didn't even have any whole milk on the countertop, only Half-and-Half.

The Basque was beloved partly for the bizarre twist of its history. The place used to be called the French Bakery back when it was owned by Francoise's immigrant parents. It took up the storefront of the town's 1930s-vintage movie palace, close by the freestanding glass ticket window, beneath the overarching neon marquee. When her father desperately needed money for surgery to replace his bad knee, the family sold the business to a Korean couple. As part of the deal, Francoise's family agreed not to open a rival bakery in or near Sonoma for five years. And so Francoise, then in her twenties, went into exile in Paris to work as an apprentice to master bakers while she waited out the years. Meanwhile the locals in Sonoma continued to patronize the French, though sometimes they snidely called it the Korean, always resentful that the founders had been driven out. As soon as the five-year prohibition was up, Francoise made her long-awaited triumphal return and opened a new café just two doors away. The locals loyally gave her their patronage, relegating the Koreans to the tourist and wholesale trades. Now in her forties, Francoise still seems absurdly youthful, with her straight black hair in a very short and aggressively stylish Parisian cut.

One of the café's walls was covered with vertical wooden racks of wine bottles. The labels were local: They were from good wineries that you could walk to from there. The Basque's wine-bar prices were ridiculously cheap. Cafés usually charge at least double the retail tag for wine, but Francoise didn't seem to have added any markup to the local favorites, as if acknowledging that you could walk up to the vines and pull off a few clusters of grapes to taste for free.

ANOTHER SONOMA INSTITUTION was Vella Cheese's old stone building where the factory space was hidden behind a small store. Ignacio "Ig" Vella was at the counter talking with a white-haired lady, a fellow septuagenarian. Ig's face had a craggy expressiveness of contour and line. He was healthy and vital but was nonetheless what the Sicilians would call "a man with a belly." His protruding stomach was actually useful in his craft. Every day, between eleven-thirty and one, Ig rolled the cheese by hand, meaning he poured the concoction of cow's milk solids and enzymes from a large vat into a cloth bag, then rolled the bag against his midsection to mold it into the shape of a wheel. After it had set, he coated the wheel with a mixture of vegetable oil and cocoa, which sealed in the flavors while allowing the cheese to breathe. Then the wheel rested on wooden storage racks for two years until it turned rock-hard and the flavors became more subtle and complex. The cheese was called dry jack, but it didn't taste at all like the softer mass-produced jacks in supermarkets. It had more in common with the great Italian and French cheeses.

Steve Jenkins, one of the foremost cheese experts in the United States and the author of *The Cheese Primer*, wrote: "Let there be a visible aura around this text, because elder statesman Ig Vella and his magnificent cheese are driving forces behind the emergence of American-made cheeses that must be ranked among the world's finest." He said that Vella's dry jack "rivals Parmigiano-Reggiano in its magnificent depth of flavor and visual appeal." As if that weren't effusive enough, he added that Ig's cheese was "truly an American treasure."

Ig Vella was a gourmand who nonetheless appeared unpretentious. He was contemptuous of foodies who spent excessively rather than shrewdly. A young man came in and asked for cheese that he could use when he made pizza.

"Do you have any mozzarella?" he asked.

"The only good stuff is the fresh Italian kind," Ig answered.

"But that's hellaciously expensive." He recommended a less costly hard cheese instead.

Turning back to the white-haired lady, Ig told her about a cheese that he recently revived when he discovered a lost recipe in his late father's papers. His father had died the previous year at age one hundred, finally passing on the business which he had founded in 1931 to Ig.

"You remember back in the thirties and forties, when people didn't have refrigerators," Ig said, sounding more reminiscent than instructive or didactic. People had iceboxes but the ice melted in the summer and the soft cheeses went bad. So Ig's father came up with a cheese that was aged for eight months until it was halfway between soft and hard. You could leave it out on the counter, and it provided a different taste than a reggiano or a dry jack. They called it *mezzo secco*, for "half dry." Ig sliced a few samples for the old woman and for me, and it was delicious. The flavor was enhanced by a sense of participating in a revived tradition, a conjured image of a lost era of iceboxes on a ninety-seven-degree day.

WHILE THE BASQUE was the locus of gossip in the early morning, Readers' Books was the place to schmooze in the afternoon. Readers' sprawled over three rooms in a nineteenth-century stone building near the Plaza and then jumped across the street into an annex for used books. The town's unofficial kibbitzer-in-chief was Andy Weinberger, who owned and ran the store along with his wife Lilla, aided by their teenage son and Andy's sister-in-law and his octogenarian father. The son, Tobias, also performed in Sonoma's circus sideshow, Oddville. His specialties included swallowing and breathing fire and lighting off firecrackers on his outstretched bare arms.

Andy Weinberger was born in the Bronx and he looked as though he would never willingly leave Manhattan's Upper West Side except to take the subway to Greenwich Village. He had studied the mysteries of the kabbalah. He played guitar in klezmer bands and jazz bands at the occasional wedding or bar mitzvah, but he hadn't had a gig since Purim. The Weinbergers were among the very few prominent Jews in the town, along with Ken Brown and whomever was the rabbi at the time. (One recent rabbi had been a homosexual, and the current one was a lesbian.)

Andy had an unusual approach to selling books. When a shopper asked for books on yoga, he said: "Pro or con?" He wasn't afraid to confront his customers over their taste in authors. He turned the bookstore into an ongoing political salon. He was annoyed by the National Rifle Association sticker at the nearby liquor store, which his employees frequented because it was the closest place for buying sundries. The sticker convinced him that the store's owner was a fascist, so some of Andy's colleagues began referring to the place as 'the fascist liquor store.'

Andy would have preferred to stay in the city but Lilla enjoyed the quiet sanctuary of country life. Lilla had launched her career as an assistant to the famed *New Yorker* writer Ved Mehta. Later she ran a women's shelter on the East Coast. She was the one who brought them to live on a chicken farm and fruit orchard in the Sonoma Mountain's foothills along with three other couples. Andy liked to call it "the kibbutz." Their own dwelling was an old barn where cows used to live.

"They're creeping down here," a female customer told Andy as he stood behind the counter next to the cash register. "Five- and six-bedroom monsters," she said with great indignation. "And people are buying them for seven figures."

I ran into Kathleen Caldwell, a transplanted Berkeleyite who scheduled the bookstore's author appearances. I said that I was planning to come to the evening of readings and performances by the Sonoma Writer's Group.

"That will be interesting," she said wryly. "Maybe you'll get to meet Hippie Chris."

"Who's Hippie Chris?"

"Hippie Chris comes to every reading, but he never buys a

book. When he came by once, Ross asked him to join us for dinner." Ross Cannard, the seventeen-year-old elder son of Bobby Cannard, Jr., and Ditty Vella, worked part-time at the bookstore.

"Chris asked, 'What are you having?' Ross said, 'Salad.' So Chris grabbed a bowl, went out and picked a bunch of weeds, and ate the weeds as his dinner."

FOR THE SONOMA WRITER'S GROUP event, the staffers at Reader's dragged away many of the annex's bookshelves to make room for a few dozen folding chairs. Every seat was taken. From the first reading, I knew that this would be unlike any event I had ever attended at a bookstore: Sharon S. Savage did a dramatic interpretation of her poem entitled "The F Word." She was so fit that it's difficult to estimate her age, but her salt-and-pepper hair suggested that she might be in her fifties. She was buxom and braless in a black Spandex top that highlighted the contours of her hard nipples. She moved aside the podium and the microphone and began sprawling over a chair as she recited her poem:

"Fearful, flayed, falling, floundering, flittering, flailing . . ."

As she enunciated each word, she shifted into yet another sensual pose.

"Flapping, floundering, flee, floating, feelings flooding, flipping, flashing, flickering, flaring, flicking . . . flaunting, flirting . . . fulfilling . . . *female!*"

Sitting next to me, a father turned to his son, who looked about twelve years old, and said in a respectful tone: "This is called 'performance art.'"

Sharon S. Savage was followed by Dick Kirk, a Sonoma native who had been a cowboy and a bull-barn cleaner. Now he was a psychiatrist.

"I was going to say something terribly sexist after Sharon's reading," he said. He paused, then he went ahead and said it: "That's a hard ass to follow."

The audience laughed loudly, as if the cowboy were the new Oscar Wilde.

After a few disappointingly conventional authors, a man named Terry NcNeely read a poem about a trip to Spain that he had taken the previous year with six fellow Sonoma poets. A chorus of the female writers chanted the repeated refrain: "The men plow the fields and look puzzled / Have thoughts and spill the coffee."

Then the white-haired Janet Wentworth read her poem "Rush":

> The Internet gold rush
> bigger, better
> take a letter
> what will happen to us?
> we're falling off the planet
> dammit

That was the entire poem. Her little verse was greeted with great applause.

Then, finally, came the return of the daring Sharon S. Savage. This time she was wearing only a white towel and had let down her long hair.

"Naked," she began, "in this misty meadow, I walk as one with the female deer." Her heroic nipples were very visibly erect. I wondered if that precocious twelve-year-old boy was developing an appreciation for the arts.

IF YOU SAW an overweight thirty-five-year-old man steer his car into the empty parking lot of a neighborhood bar before ten in the morning and sit there alone, waiting impatiently for the doors to open so he could be the first customer and quickly finish a couple of drinks and then spend the rest of the late spring day (sunny and dry and pleasantly warm at seventy-six degrees) slogging off to a series of other nearby bars, you might think that the solitary man was a potential alcoholic and view him with a mixture of sympathy and scorn. But if you didn't call the places "bars" and instead referred to them as the "tasting rooms" or "visitor centers" of well-reputed wineries in a renowned vineyard area, you would probably view the drinker with admiration and envy as an enthusiast, a connoisseur, an aesthete, a gourmand, a bon vivant, a lover of the good life, a man of refined tastes and sensibilities, or at least an eager tourist.

So that was me—an enthusiast, mind you, not a drunk—at ten in the morning at the Ravenswood winery, a rustic stone structure at the rocky base of the green hills to the northeast of town. The space had an airy, light-splashed California style, with large windows looking toward the dozen acres of vines surfing up and down the steep slopes. The walls were hung with black-and-white photographs of fans who had the Ravenswood logo tattooed on various parts of their bodies. The insignia looked like an abstract design at first, but was actually a drawing of three blackbirds inside a circular medallion. One of the photos showed a woman with the logo etched directly above her ample breast. Another groupie, named Misty, posed gamely in unbuttoned blue jeans and a bare midriff to show off the raven logo tattoo on her skinny tummy. This snapshot was displayed rather discreetly inside the men's restroom.

Back in the main room, on the bar, a picture postcard showed a bunch of naked guys inside wine barrels. The balding man in the center—he was the head winemaker, actually—waved his arms frantically as though he were drowning.

The Sonoma Valley's wine people cultivated a wackiness and subversive irreverence to counter the haughty pretentiousness and overblown egotism they considered the hallmark of their rivals on the other side of the Mayacamas in the Napa Valley. And at Ravenswood the wine itself reflected this defiantly down-home attitude. The vineyard was well known for zinfandel, a grape that had become popular in California. It wasn't one of the classic grapes of old Europe, like cabernet sauvignon or chardonnay, that gave an advantage to the French because they had a head start of a thousand years.

An American vintner specializing in zin instead of cab was like a classically trained pastry chef whose signature dish was her grandma's country apple pie rather than tarte tatin or crème brûlée. She couldn't affect a snobbery and she had to forgo the gratification of having her creations compared directly with those of the French masters. Nonetheless, she made something that was beloved and delicious.

Winery tasting rooms had a strange culture. The traveling gourmands who frequented them assumed that the wine pourers shared their own well-heeled and highly educated backgrounds. The visitors treated their hosts behind the counter with considerable respect and even a certain reverence for their knowledge about a chronically complex and sometimes dauntingly arcane field. After all, the winery's staffers were always chatting so authoritatively about the virtues of malolactic fermentation for making chardonnay more supple or the reasons for growing particular varieties of grapes in certain microclimates or the differences between aging wine in French oak barrels versus American ones.

How pleasurably ironic to think that the wine snobs of the haute bourgeoisie paid such deference to people who lived in trailer parks in the Springs, where they fed the deer that come down from the hills as though they were the most common household pets, or in downscale apartment complexes on the west side, where the ornery tenants raised chickens on their patios. The plutocrats with their Princeton degrees and their Harvard MBAs and their law partnerships and their managing directorships—could they ever imagine that they were making pilgrimages to listen to trailer people? Did those overclass professionals know that they were trading oenophilic insights with low-wage hourly employees who were working to pay the rent on backwoods shacks?

The irony was especially sweet because the locals really knew their wines. The Ivy Leaguers flaunted their connoisseurship as proof of their intellectual aptitude and their rarified sensibility, but those trailer dwellers could talk the talk just as well even though they didn't spend a hundred grand for fancy degrees.

As I continued my tour of Sonoma's tasting rooms and went from Ravenswood to the nearest winery, Bartholomew Park, I had to return to the flat plain of the valley floor and then fork off the rectilinear grid and onto narrow roads that curve through wondrously fragrant eucalyptus and great old oaks as they climb back to the hills. The roads are lined with single-story ranch-style homes, their small lots covered not with green lawns but rather with exposed brown soil and row after row of trellised vines. The scene was reminiscent of the old houses near the airport in Los Angeles that still have the seesaw swings of oil wells pumping away rhythmically in their tiny yards.

At the Bartholemew Park tasting room, one wall was covered from floor to ceiling with black-and-white photographs of the men and women who grew grapes and made wines in the Sonoma Valley. The shots showed couples standing naked behind farm tractors or raising glasses above the bubbling waters of hot tubs. Nearby the winery stood the white mansion of the vineyard's founder, the self-proclaimed "Baron" Auguston Haraszthy, a Hungarian hustler who pretended to be a nobleman. He raised the capital to build his wine empire by embezzling from the U.S. mint in San Francisco. With the stolen cash he went into partnership with an equally shrewd operator, Mariano Vallejo. After 1846, when the gringos revolted against Mexico and raised the Bear Flag on Sonoma's Plaza, creating the Republic of California, Vallejo morphed from colonial potentate to American robber baron. His venture with Haraszthy inaugurated northern California's wine business, born of rogues and robbery.

WHEN I FIRST CAME TO SONOMA, I saw a posting on the front door of the Meritage restaurant for a "winemakers' dinner," a $100-a-person extravaganza with six food courses paired with ten different Sonoma Valley wines. The vintners themselves would be there to talk about their creations. I didn't hesitate to make a reservation, and I was surprised that there were still places. If that kind of event were held in San Francisco, it might sell out even before the advertisements ran in the paper. But in the hinterlands, on a Tuesday night, when all of the weekend people were back in the city, a marathon hundred-bucks-a-plate dinner wasn't a draw. Everyone else there knew each other. They were all connected to the wineries represented tonight. I was the only outsider at an insiders' gathering, an accidental spy of their subculture.

The evening's emcee was Lance Cutler, who for more than a decade was the winemaker at Gundlach-Bundschu, one of the oldest wineries in Sonoma. At his signal the dinner guests found seats. It was like a game of musical chairs, and when the music stopped, I was the loser. Everyone else was seated with their cronies and I was still left standing. Eventually I found the one open seat. A good-looking middle-aged Italian-American couple was next to me. The woman was a fake blonde in a short, tight black skirt and a halter top that showed off her bustline and her tan lines. The man was dark-haired and mustachioed. He looked fit in slacks and a sportshirt. He had a mischievous glint and a swaggering vitality.

The emcee launched into a stand-up comedy routine about their business.

"When you have lunch with a Napa winemaker," he said, "it has to be over by three o'clock so he has time to get to the bank. When you have lunch with a Sonoma winemaker, you try to get home before it's dark outside!"

The crowd laughed because the joke reflected their cherished self-perception, the idea that they were in this for their genuine love of wine and food and camaraderie, while the snobby Napa egoists were in it for the money.

The emcee proclaimed that tonight we were going to hear anecdotes about the art of winemaking, and he called first on Joey Benziger of Benziger Vineyards, a large and prosperous operation in Glen Ellen.

The dark-haired macho man left our table and stepped forward.

He was Joey Benziger. He began to tell his tale with a bravura narrative style that suggested he had had a lifetime of experience holding forth at crowded bars. It was a story about his late father, Bruno, who moved the family from New York, where they had a successful liquor business, to Sonoma, where they wanted desperately to develop a reputation for making outstanding wines. Bruno showed great enthusiasm for a vintage that was fermenting in the tank. It was going to be his first "reserve" wine, a supposedly superior offering destined to excite the critics, command high prices, and make a vineyard's name. But then one day a hapless worker had a collision while driving the forklift. He punctured the tank and spilled the hundreds of gallons of liquid onto the floor of the winery. They had to dump it all in the creek, furtively violating the environmental regulations.

The terrified forklift driver was brought into the office of Bruno Benziger, who was a former military officer and a legendary tough guy. The boss stared angrily at the employee. Then Bruno reached into a drawer, pulled out a loaded revolver, and placed it on the top of his desk, right in front of the worker.

"You know the honorable thing to do," Bruno told him.

That was the punchline to Joey's anecdote, and it elicited loud laughter and a few hoots and catcalls from the crowd at the restaurant, where everyone was already intoxicated. Obviously satisfied with his performance, Joey returned to the table, happy and energized. He thrust his hand toward me.

"I'm Joey Benziger," he said. "Who are you?"

"I'm writing a book about the wine country."

"Holy shit!" he exclaimed, recoiling, visibly terrified that he had just screwed up by telling that story. But then his tenseness gave way and he flashed a smile that said what-the-hell, what-me-worry, who-really-gives-a-damn.

The meal began with Maine lobster salad with heirloom tomatoes, avocado, and grapefruit in a citrus chive dressing, then continued with pan-seared sea scallops stuffed with local Sonoma foie gras and drizzled with white truffle oil and caviar sauce. Then there was duck prosciutto topped with baby artichokes, asparagus, and aged Vella cheese, and risotto with fresh morel mushrooms in a cabernet sauvignon sauce, and strips of grilled venison and lamb loin artfully braided together and topped with a wild berry sauce.

With course after course the winemakers drank and had a bois-terous good time and told stories about other occasions when they drank and had a boisterous good time. The other couple at our table were Mary Sullivan, the winemaker for Sebastiani, and her husband, Bob, an accountant. Mary was what used to be referred to admiringly as a "dame" or a "broad." She was feminine but could hold her own with the boys when they drank and joked. She told tales of her business trips to the wine regions of France, when she would constantly make apologies for being tired, when she was actually hung over. We talked about how there used to be a raucous Hell's Angels bar in Glen Ellen, and how it was a good thing the bar burned down before the rowdy Benziger boys arrived in town or surely there would have been big trouble.

The emcee called another vintner to the floor. Mike Berthoud came across as a blue-collar guy, regular and unpretentious. He talked about winemaking as an honest trade he picked up from his family, as though he were following his father and becoming a plumber or electrician or carpenter. It just happened that his father was French, his own real name was Michel (though he went by "Mike" because the French sounds like Michelle), and he was the winemaker for Arrowood, which was revered by the enthusiasts and the magazines as one of the two or three best wine labels from the Sonoma Valley.

The oenophiles at my table never made a specific critique about what they were drinking. They might say something polite to the winemaker—"this is really good"—but they never talked the usual wine talk about the tannins and the acidity and the balance and the finish and the oakiness and whether the aroma they were picking up was blackberry or black currant. They drank the wine avidly, and they enjoyed it immensely. But even though wine was their passion and their profession, and they all had highly sensitive palates and noses, they didn't show off with virtuosic displays of language and lingo the way many of their customers might have. They just enjoyed the wine and how it complemented the food.

When so many wines were being poured and it all added up rather quickly and effortlessly to a great amount of alcohol, there was no expectation that you would drink it all. The etiquette only required that every wine be tasted, not drained. But Joey Benziger seemed to clean out every glass as a matter of honor, and the other winemakers consumed far more than mere polite tasting required.

No one seemed upset when I knocked over a glass and spilled merlot all over the tablecloth. I sensed that I could spill red wine on any of them and it would be all right. Then somebody said that the sun was setting, and everyone dropped their silverware and rushed outside to see the spectacle.

Under the influence of the booze, the wine people become very physical. They were grabbing and slapping and high-fiving. Diane Benziger reminisced about how she was such a bad girl in Catholic high school. Joey Benziger laughed about how he once tried with all his might to push his brother off a twenty-foot-high stairway banister. Diane recalled how the locals all eyed them suspiciously when they came to Glen Ellen, and how she and her mother-in-law won over their neighbors by cooking them Italian dinners nearly every night

As midnight neared and the dessert finally arrived—warm chocolate tortes with hazelnut gelato—there was a chorus of cliches like "screw the damn cholesterol" and "you've gotta live while you can," and everyone ate it all.

AFTER THAT DINNER I began hearing stories about Lance Cutler, our emcee that evening. Lance was almost single-handedly responsible for turning the natural rivalry between the Sonoma and

Napa valleys into an epic feud. He was the person who promoted the idea that Napa was blighted by overblown egos and rampant greed and grandiose self-importance while Sonoma was about down-home informality and wacky irreverent humor and a playful subversive spirit.

Lance was Sonoma's belated answer to Napa's Robert Mondavi. He was a promoter who resorted to guerrilla tactics to attract the media attention to his own cause. Lance was the mastermind of publicity stunts such as the hijacking of the Napa Valley Wine Train. The train was a successful tourist gimmick: Visiting connoisseurs sat in refurbished old-time cars and enjoyed Napa wines with a gourmet dinner as they chugged along looking out at the vineyards. Lance hijacked the train so he could expose the passengers to Sonoma wines—and get lots of headlines. Similarly, Lance's troops invaded Mustard's, a popular restaurant on the floor of the Napa Valley, during the busiest hour of Saturday dinner, handing out blue-stemmed glasses, which were a hallmark of Sonoma, and pouring Sonoma wines. Then, in his most audacious escapade, Lance hijacked a bus carrying the British billionaire Richard Branson, the founder of the Virgin airline and retail empire, who was on his way to visit wineries in the rival valley. As Branson's entourage made its way up from San Francisco, Lance's men descended in helicopters and on motorcycles and horses to blockade the path and then redirect the bus to the Gundlach-Bundschu winery, where Lance forced his hostages to taste wines from Sonoma rather than Napa. Branson, himself a fervent hypester who had done everything from ballooning and parachuting to dressing in drag to promote his own businesses, was charmed by the stunt.

I heard so much about Lance's exploits that I called him and asked if we could get together. He told me to show up at his house at eleven-thirty for lunch. I drove past the taco stands and bodegas of the Springs and turned off the main road at an abandoned old brick building that looked like it might have been a saloon during the Wild West days. The road led into a densely wooded area in the foothills of the Mayacamas. Lance's yellow-painted wooden cottage was built into the slope of a hillside. The structure was very small, less than a thousand square feet, with a large covered porch in the front that ran the width of the house. Lance was sitting on the porch with Claude Berthoud, an old French winemaker. They were both holding red wine glasses, a few sips remaining in them, and sitting beside a bottle of Claude's wine, which was nearly empty. Hardly eleven-thirty, and they had already finished a bottle.

Lance served a gewurztraminer with a chopped celery salad from the current *Saveur* with a platter of spicy Italian meats and good fresh bread. His wife, Sandy, joined us at the table of glass and cast iron on the covered terrace.

"I was a teacher in East L.A. and Watts," Lance said. "Every time I saved a thousand dollars, we left and traveled. When we first came to Sonoma in the seventies, it was all hippies and redneck farmers and Mexicans. In the seventies if there was a deer on your property here, you would shoot it and eat it. Today, if there's a deer on your property, you shoot it and you get arrested."

He learned winemaking by making his own wine here at his cottage in the Springs, and he took a couple of three-day courses at the University of California at Davis, which was about an hour's drive away. With this limited training, he went to work at Gundlach-Bundschu in 1981. Gundlach was an expansive old farm at the eastern edge of the valley, about two miles beyond the village, and it had a winery that dated back to the nineteenth century. But it hadn't made wine for decades, not since one of the family's matriarchs joined the temperance movement. After World War II the Bundschus, an old German dynasty, began growing grapes for the Sebastianis, the town's great Italian winemaking dynasty. And after the scion Jim Bundschu graduated from Berkeley in the 1960s, he decided to revive the family's own wine label. He hired Lance as his winemaker, and Lance quickly took on the role of promoter-provocateur as well. He became known as a joker, especially when he duped a reporter for the *Index-Tribune* about his supposed plans to build a retractable dome over Gundlach-Bundschu's vineyards to shield them from unwanted rains late in the season. The newspaper's editors were embarrassed when they had to print a retraction.

Lance faced the promotional challenge of having to inform people about how to pronounce the winery's difficult name, which the Bundschus insisted on keeping as an homage to their ancestors and a continuation of a long tradition. So Lance came up with a poster with four images: a gun, a lock, a bun, and a shoe—*gun lock bun shoe* being a close phonetic approximation of the moniker. This initial effort led to a series of several dozen promotional posters with stagy photography and wacky humor. For his most notorious effort, Lance assembled a throng of townspeople in front of Sonoma's city hall, held a free two-hour wine tasting to create a celebratory mood, and then had them strike funny and exuberant poses for the photographer while they were holding two bottles of wine apiece, which were supposed to represent their average daily consumption.

"Two bottles a day—that's all we ask!" ran the poster's prominent caption. The broadsheet was instantly beloved in the village and the valley, becoming a popular collector's item. But it evoked public opposition from the town's police force, which claimed that Lance was encouraging drunkenness, and at city hall, no less. Even worse, a bunch of minors had been included in the poster.

"The cops all live outside Sonoma, and they have a bad attitude toward the town," he said. "People have been arrested here for drunk bicycling, drunk horse riding. Even drunk walking when they're walking home from the Plaza!"

Ever since he left Gundlach-Bundschu, weary of having to hold an everyday job, he continued concocting his own vintages. For most garage winemakers, the first problem is securing a supply of any grapes, let alone top-quality ones. Lance's gimmick was that he approached the best of the grape growers who sell their harvests by the ton to other vintners rather than making their own wines. These growers needed a way of showing off the flavors and potential of their fruit to prospective buyers. So they hired Lance to make and bottle relatively small batches of wine for them, which became their equivalent of product samples. He got to keep some of the bottles for his own cellar.

Lance looked across his yard toward the cottage next door.

"A gay couple and a lesbian couple from the city bought that house," he said. "It cost a million dollars total: six hundred thousand to buy it, and three hundred to fix it up, and another hundred to buy the adjacent lot. A million dollars for a *weekend* place!" Looking at the remarkably humble, undistinguished, small structure, it was easy to understand his bewilderment. Lance's neighborhood wasn't in a fancy part of town. He was in the barrio, the last refuge of the immigrant farmworkers and the artsy bohemians. Now the gentrifiers from the city were arriving, but they still hadn't figured out what life here was really about. "I offered them plum-tree wood from my yard for their smoker," Lance said, "but they insisted on buying fruitwood in the store!"

We laughed aloud and finished off two bottles of pinot noir as the lunch hour turned into mid-afternoon. Lance opened a chardonnay from a famous Sonoma vineyard, but he wasn't thrilled by the taste, so we abandoned it after consuming only half its contents. Lance held up his glass and flicked his wrist so the remaining wine went flying in a forceful parabolic trajectory over the railing of the porch, and he watched as it sprinkled the green shrubbery. He tried a petite syrah from California, which he enjoyed, but then came a bottle of Bordeaux, which "sucked" in his estimation, and it too wound up fertilizing the lawn. Then a very expensive bottle of Napa Cabernet received the same fate.

Around five o'clock Claude reluctantly left to drive into town because he was scheduled to play a *petanque* match against another Sonoma vintner. Lance lingered over a final bottle of syrah, talking about his new career as a writer. Since leaving Gundlach-Bundschu, Lance had started his own small press and written and published books about winemaking and about tequila, another of his passions. He didn't make much money from his personal press, which sold only a few thousand copies of each book. But he had a lifestyle that gave him great freedom to work on whatever he wanted, whenever he wanted to, and to spend warm afternoons outside talking and eating and drinking with his friends.

"The number one thing that I'm about isn't writing," he said. "It's lunches and dinners like this on my porch." He was offered $50,000 by one of the big booze companies to go on a nationwide tour to talk about tequila, but he turned down the offer because having to leave his porch wasn't worth fifty grand to him, even though that was much more than his annual income. He said that he had lived in this house for more than twenty years, and he paid only $550 a month in rent, which was very inexpensive, less than half of what you would pay for a one-room studio apartment in San Francisco those days. But now that Sonoma was being invaded by richer types, like his new neighbors, he was about to lose his lease, and he dreaded that he would have to get a real job again. Lance Cutler, as much as anyone, represented *la vie bohème* in Sonoma, and if he was forced to abandon his cherished porch, that lifestyle would have suffered a sad defeat.

At six-thirty Lance needed to leave for a dinner appointment. And so, after seven hours and nine bottles of wine, a memorable lunch was ending.

SONOMA'S CULTURE AND CHARACTER—the appealingly human scale, the enviable harmony of the small town and the natural surroundings, the encouraging sense of community at the Plaza and the café and the bookstore and the farmer's market and the movie palace and the cheese shop—were rare in contemporary America and worth preserving. The struggle for Sonoma's soul didn't start with the chickens, and it wouldn't end there, either. I wasn't surprised to learn that it had begun with the same man whose bravura presentation had helped to rally the chicken supporters to victory: Tom Whitworth.

The cradle of Tom's revolution was an unlikely spot called Murphy's. The town of Sonoma had a number of restaurants that were written about adoringly in the *New York Times* and served as enviable destinations for expensive culinary pilgrimages, but Murphy's was not among them. It was possible but unlikely that an outsider would venture into Murphy's, even by accident. Murphy's was close to the town square, where the visitors parked their Porsches and BMWs and Mercedes, but it was well hidden. You had to walk through one of the long alleyways—or, more lyrically, the *paseos* (passages), as they were called by the town's nineteenth-century Spanish colonialists. At first all you'd see were the bowels of Francoise's bakery, where baguettes cooled on racks. Then you'd see the high barren concrete side wall of the old-time movie palace. You would think that this was a service corridor. Actually, it was where the locals liked to hide.

Murphy's was a classic Irish pub with dark wooden walls hung with the kitschy mirrors that the breweries provided as free ornamentation. It served pub food that was authentically mediocre, unhealthy, and cheap. No one came to Murphy's because they craved fine cuisine, and a few people probably regretted the Irish stew they ordered to counterbalance their pints of dark Guinness stout. But Murphy's was beloved for its hominess and its warmth and its insider ethos.

Murphy's was a hangout for the local politicos. The owner himself, Larry Murphy, had served as the town's mayor. During his term of office, he had been arrested for driving while intoxicated, a legendary incident that endeared him to the village's habitual drinkers. The leaders of Sonoma's Democratic Party assembled in Murphy's private back room to decide on their candidates and their platforms.

So it was oddly appropriate when, one night in the fall of 1999, Tom's cabal of local activists began to gather there too. Their grassroots movement was made up of artists and poets and environmentalists and pamphleteers and a reclusive importer of handmade Egyptian rugs and a hippie chick named Jewel who taught "ecstatic dance" at the community center.

Together these ragtag bohemians—a bunch of iconoclasts and eccentrics who mostly had fled the big cities—were taking on the homegrown Babbitts, the laissez-faire small-town boosters they referred to derisively as the "Old Guard."

They were trying to keep their elected officials from selling out the town to the forces of money and influence. They were defying an entrenched establishment. They were attempting a radical experiment in direct democracy.

And, astonishingly, it looked like they had a chance of winning.

They were officially named the Sonoma Hillside Preservation Alliance, but they liked to call themselves the Yes Group, since they were for a vote of yes on Measure A, the referendum that they had passed around petitions for and signed and gotten put on the ballot. The "Yes" name was misleading because their message was actually a defiant no to the invasion of wealthy outsiders. Measure A would prevent the city council from allowing a real-estate developer to put up a luxurious hotel and resort on a virgin hillside.

The proposed site was extraordinarily sensitive: The hillside slated for development was prominent in the astonishing scenic backdrop framing the city hall and town square as you drove on Broadway, the main thoroughfare that ran into town and through its center.

The Plaza was Sonoma's formal front yard—the place where it greeted and entertained its visitors, a meticulously landscaped and manicured park lined by restaurants and shops. The hill was Sonoma's backyard. It was a patch of wild greenery that only the locals frequented. Even then, intransigent hikers had to bushwhack through dense layers of poison oak that covered the floor of a forest of coastal live oak trees and fragrant eucalyptus and gave way to meadows of unruly tall grasses and wildflowers trampled by deer and wild turkeys.

The hill lay behind the everyday places where outsiders rarely wandered: the Little League fields and the *petanque* courts and the Veterans Hall and the parking lot where the farmer's market was held on Friday mornings. It was the closest thing the town had to sacred ground: The sixty-acre plot that the developers wanted so badly was right next to the historic nineteenth-century cemetery, which held the tomb of the town's founder, Mexican general Mariano Vallejo, and the ancestors of many old families still in Sonoma. (The cemetery was also where Stefan, the vampire man, who wore the same pair of black velvet tights every day, held Neo-Danz, midnight dance performances inspired by themes from the occult.)

The Yes activists forcefully proposed an alternative to a resort hotel for elite outsiders. They wanted to build a hiking trail to preserve the hillside's natural beauty and to ensure that it remained easily and freely accessible. The trail would maintain the site as a common resource shared by all of Sonoma's residents. It would be "minimally intrusive" to the environment, they said. To be sure, some scarlike gashes of red volcanic soil would be exposed when they sliced away acres of poison oak and cut zigzagging pathways. But new vegetation would quickly grow alongside the trail to hide it from sight. When they viewed the hillside from the valley below, the residents would still enjoy the same awestruck panorama and feel the same sense of living amid undisturbed nature. They wouldn't be forced into the indignity of looking up at Olympian plutocrats who played tennis or discussed deals poolside while they sneered down at the poorer locals.

To the bohemians the controversy was the crucial test of whether the town of Sonoma would become just another playground for rich visitors or whether it would serve the people who had made their lives there. They feared sharing the fate of Carmel on California's central coast. Carmel had begun as a haven of modest seaside cottages for artists and writers. Eventually the area turned into a prohibitively expensive enclave of trophy houses for the rich, and overpriced boutiques and kitsch emporiums for daytrippers.

They didn't want Sonoma to be "Carmelized," they said, conjuring images of the town cooking slowly until it turned overly sweet. They dreaded attracting evil megalomaniacal power brokers from New York and Hollywood—as either part-time residents or real-estate developers—and becoming "Hamptonized." And most importantly they didn't want the Sonoma Valley to become the new Napa Valley. But now someone was trying to give them a 105-room resort in a class with Meadowood, where the Napa Valley Wine Auction threw its annual orgy of conspicuous consumption. The new hotel would rival Napa's Auberge du Soleil, where the bar was filled with men in Armani suits and starlet types in black cocktail dresses and strappy sandals with four-inch spike heels.

The reputation of the developer, Rosewood Hotels and Resorts, implied that the pleasure dome on the Sonoma hillside would host a social scene that was at least as fabulously wealthy, and perhaps even more rarified and baronial. Rosewood's thirteen properties gave substance to the cliché of "world class." The chain included several leading hotels in major cities worldwide, most famously the Carlyle in Manhattan with its graceful Art Deco tower overlooking Central Park. Rosewood ran the Lanesborough in London, a landmark 1828 hotel on the corner of Hyde Park. And it owned Hotel Seiyo Ginza at the center of Tokyo's notorious neon-lit shopping boulevard. The Seiyo offered full maid service *twice* a day. Rosewood also operated two hotels in Dallas, where it was based, including the Mansion on Turtle Creek, which had one of America's most famous restaurants.

Rosewood seemed to follow its moneyed clientele wherever they traveled for privileged pleasure as well as for global business. It owned Bandrutt's Palace in St. Moritz, an 1896 mansion near the ski slopes of the Swiss Alps. It ran Caneel Bay on St. John, which was ensconced within the five-thousand-acre Virgin Islands National Park on a beach that had been owned by the Rockefellers; Little Dix Bay, which it called a "boutique resort," in the British Virgin Islands; the King Pacific Lodge, a "remote wilderness retreat" in British Columbia; and Las Ventanas al Paraiso in Los Cabos, Mexico.

To the Sonoma bohemians, though, the most suspicious fact about Rosewood was its holdings in the Persian Gulf, which made the company seem like a coconspirator with the imperialist powers controlling the world's precious natural resources. Rosewood's slickly produced website trumpeted Al Faisaliah in the capital city of Riyadh as "the most luxurious hotel in the Kingdom—setting new standards of elegance and service in Saudi Arabia" with "the only 24-hour butler service in the Middle East." The Royal Suite went for $1,500 a night. Rosewood also ran Hotel Al Khozama (for "sweet desert flower") in Riyadh, "an oasis of comfort blossoming in the desert" with a "greater than 2 to 1 staff-to-guest ratio," and the Dharmarangsa in Jakarta in Islamic, oil-rich Indonesia.

Rosewood's return customers weren't just the nouveaux riches of America; it had a following among the world's ruling classes: the Arab petro-barons and the decadent remnants of the European aristocracy and the rest of the elusive elite. And the bohemians were especially incensed by the rumor that Rosewood planned to fly in its customers by *helicopter* from Silicon Valley and the San Francisco airport.

Helicopter!

When Rosewood came to Sonoma, its first critical mistake—the action that made it seem nefarious—was to talk in private with members of the city council about making a deal for the hillside land, which belonged to the town.

Tom Whitworth heard about this and he was outraged. It seemed that Rosewood was treating little Sonoma as if it were another one of the Developing World backwaters where it built sumptuous resorts. The developer had sought out the oligarchs who supposedly ruled the place, as if this were Saudi Arabia! They were ignoring the will of the people.

After five years of living in Sonoma, Tom felt a profound affection for the place, but he despised what he characterized as the know-nothings who ran it. He had gone to several of the public fortnightly meetings of the five-member city council, which seemed sadly weak and unquestioning in its support of the business community. Tom was especially annoyed and frustrated by the mayor, a sixtysomething small-time businessman who epitomized the Old Guard. "He was a fool," Tom later told me. "An idiot. And his idiocy was becoming offensive."

And so, when Tom heard that the elected officials were meeting secretly with the Rosewood developers, he went to city hall and obtained a copy of California's Brown Act, which made it illegal for even two of the local representatives to get together anywhere without posting public notification in advance and following a number of careful requirements.

Tom spoke at a council meeting, demanding redress and open discussion. And he published a public letter to the mayor with his unexpurgated criticisms.

"People were shocked that someone like me could write something so vicious in a town where everyone had always been so nice to each other," he recalled.

The battle was on.

Tom helped to found the Yes Group, and his key allies included a couple of cheese brokers. Gary Edwards was a slender, intense man who looked like Timothy Busfield from television's *Thirtysomething* with a balding pate and reddish hair. He was the owner of Sage Marketing, a three-person operation that arranged for supermarket chains to take wholesale orders from some of the finest small cheesemakers in America. His colleague in the business was his lover Maria "Ditty" Vella, as in the doo-wop song riff "doo ah–ditty ditty-dum ditty-dum." She was the third generation of Sonoma's cheesemaking dynasty. The Vellas were an almost universally well-known and beloved old family in Sonoma. Ditty, who was born in the town and had spent her entire life in the Sonoma Valley, gave their opposition movement an invaluable credibility with her fellow natives.

Ditty was Ig Vella's daughter, though politically they were very far apart. During the decades that he spent waiting to inherit the family business, Ig became a force in Sonoma politics. He was elected to the board of supervisors that ran the county. He was part of the Old Guard, the old business-as-usual crowd, one of the en-trenched power brokers that activists like Ditty were now trying so hard to dethrone.

Sonoma was divided into the bohemians, who mostly were transplants, and the natives, who tended to be either small-town Babbitts or farm country shitkickers. Ditty Vella was akin to roy-alty among the shitkickers, too. She had lived for many years with her husband, Robert "Bobby" Cannard, Jr. (son of Bob Cannard, Sr., the chicken farmer), on their own organic farm on Sonoma Mountain, going from town to town to sell fresh vegetables at farmer's markets. It was a precarious existence. Their lucky break came when the legendary Alice Waters went on a search for an or-ganic farm that could reliably provide much of the produce for her Berkeley restaurant, Chez Panisse.

Alice visited the family on the mountain and discovered that their younger son was named Marius, which was also the name of the title character in a novel by the French author Marcel Pagnol. Alice Waters was a fervent admirer of Pagnol, the bard of her beloved Provence. She named her own daughter Fanny after an-other one of Pagnol's characters. And the movie poster of *Marius* hangs in the upstairs bar and café of her restaurant. So when she met Ditty's son, she took his name as a sign that this was the right farm for her. She gave them a contract with generous terms, trans-forming their idealistic pursuit from a risky proposition into a sta-ble business for the long run.

Bobby was a charismatic proselytizer for organic agriculture. He was Johnny Appleseed for the New Age. The course he taught for many years at the community college inspired and trained a generation of farmers, who spread the organic movement through Sonoma. But his passion for the natural bordered on the fanatical. Ditty clashed with him when he refused to let her take their sons to get braces to straighten their teeth. He argued that anything that restricted the flow of air into the mouth would inhibit the natural growth of the children. Eventually Ditty divorced him, came down from the mountain, and moved away a few miles, back to the village on the valley floor where she had grown up. She lived in a tiny cottage behind the Vella cheese factory and began a long-term relationship with Gary Edwards, a Sonoma County native who had learned the cheese business from many late nights—sometimes three or four a week—drinking brandy with Ditty's nonagenarian grandfather.

Tom Whitworth and Gary Edwards began assailing the city council over the proposed hotel development in the summer of 1998, but found the members eager for the tax revenues and attention that the Rosewood resort would bring to the town.

The opposition's first hope came in the November election, when Ken Brown, a charismatic bohemian who had a ponytail that hung down to his waist, won a seat on the council.

Ken was a Jewish New Yorker, a native of the borough of Queens. When he returned from the war in Vietnam, he hitch-hiked around America and slept on the beaches of southern California for a while. He eventually returned to Gotham and drove a taxicab on the late-night shift in the early seventies, much like the Robert DeNiro character in the film *Taxi Driver* (though without becoming a homicidal maniac). Ken ascribed the city's dramatic decline to the bad influence of his fellow Vietnam vets, who either terrorized Central Park with muggings—"which were inspired by guerrilla warfare with the Viet Cong," he claimed—or became rogue cops corrupted by the drug trade, as in *The French Connection.*

In 1974 he fled to California to get out of a failed relationship and came to the Sonoma Valley, where two of his ex-girlfriends were living. Within two weeks he found work at a winery as a grape picker and then as a "cellar rat," a manual laborer who hooked up hoses and maneuvered forklifts.

When Ken Brown first came to the town of Sonoma, a lot of its people still got around on horseback, and there was a feed store at the corner of the Plaza where you could buy ducks or pull up your pickup and load it with grain.

He spent five years as a cellar rat and married a local woman who wrote poetry. They paid $45 a month to live in a trailer until his wife became pregnant and the space literally wasn't wide enough for her to make her way through. He became the caretaker at the community center, living in the former principal's office of the converted red-brick school building and looking after the art and dance studios and the eighty merlot vines lining the parking lot. Eventually he rose to events director of the institution and became a very visible and popular figure in the village. He even got away with having the center host a performance by the Explicit Players, an avantgarde Berkeley theater troupe–cum–commune that practiced and advocated illegal public nudity.

The civil servants at city hall were openly alarmed when this hippie (albeit an aging one) with a long ponytail narrowly defeated an Old Guard pro-business booster named Dick Dorf—maliciously nicknamed Dick Dork by the bohemians—for a seat on the city council. Ken joined with the Yes Group and bolstered their efforts to reclaim the town.

One other city council member opposed the Rosewood resort: Larry Barnett, like Tom Whitworth, was another dropout from corporate America who prized the small-town feeling and the sense of community in Sonoma. He had been the chief executive officer of a sizable publicly traded company in Silicon Valley in the eighties before he came to town and bought the Thistle Dew Inn, a bed-and-breakfast with just a few rooms in a modest old bungalow a block away from the Plaza.

But these two bohemians on the city council were outweighed by the three members from the Old Guard, and they couldn't prevent the majority from selling out to Rosewood. So the resort's opponents began gathering signatures to put the issue to a voter referendum in a special election. Ultimately they collected seven hundred names. They went to the farmer's market with an open water jug for donations, garnering fives and tens from many of their neighbors.

The de facto headquarters of the Yes Group, a.k.a. the Sonoma Hillside Preservation Alliance, was Gary and Ditty's cheese brokerage, Sage Marketing, a little one-story yellow shingled cottage that had been built a century earlier as the town's first library. Their political rivals were based only a half-block away, at the corner of the Plaza, in Modern Eve, a costly boutique that sold slinky sundresses and designer sportswear and appealed to well-heeled visitors from out of town. The store's owner, Alexis Gray, was the leader of the movement for a vote of no on Measure A, which was formally called Sonoma Citizens for Responsible Planning.

Within the self-contained universe that Sonoma represented in the minds of its residents, this was akin to the Republican and Democratic national parties operating out of adjacent suites in the Watergate Hotel.

Alexis Gray was in her early thirties and she was married, but she still dressed like a flirtatious teenager. She wore a metallic necklace that said "Alexis" and drew the eye toward her chest. She favored clingy low-cut dresses that showed off her buxom figure with bravado. Many of the local men found her sexy, but Gary Edwards sneered that "she looks like a prostitute." He speculated that she was merely a figurehead for the behind-the-scenes powers that were promoting the hillside development, whom he believed must have promised her a boutique concession in the resort hotel. He was suspicious of her partly because she lived not in the homey village itself but way over in Diamond A, a string of trophy houses that had replaced an old cattle ranch in the mountains above the western edge of the valley. The bohemians at their most paranoid speculated that Diamond A was a haven for illicit eighties drug money.

"She's the epitome of what this town is not," Gary told me. "She's what I don't want to see in this town."

The campaign was acrimonious. The bohemians believed that

the Babbitts were blatantly, systematically—and illegally—removing the yellow Yes signs and stickers that they had placed conspicuously around town. Tom claimed that he actually saw Hal Beck, the director of the chamber of commerce and official spokesman for Sonoma's business interests, stealing a Yes magnet from a car parked near the Plaza. What actually happened will remain controversial. But in Tom's vivid description of the scene, he made frantic pursuit. Hal ducked into Modern Eve, the safe haven for his side, but Tom risked an incursion into the forbidding enemy territory.

Hal denied removing the magnet.

Tom said: "That's chickenshit."

Hal challenged whether Tom was even a citizen. He demanded to see Tom's green card. The police finally arrived and separated them. The town's newspaper, the Sonoma *Index-Tribune*, reported how there had "nearly been fistfights" between the opponents in the acrimonious Measure A campaign.

The Yes activists raised more than $10,000, but they were massively outspent, more than ten to one, by the moneyed interests. The bohemians were terrified of losing, and they responded with an impressive display of energy and public presence. They held rallies and stayed proudly visible throughout the town in Yes T-shirts and badges. They were appalled when they heard that the business lobby was entertaining the town police officers to ask for their support. The Babbitts were saying that without the extra tax revenues from the resort, Sonoma wouldn't have enough money for its cops, conjuring images of a peaceful small town suddenly going to hell.

After a summer of intense campaigning, the town held a special election on September 21, 1999. The bohemians gathered and jumped in the air in front of city hall to celebrate their efforts whatever the outcome and drank their pints at Murphy's—and heard, astonishingly, that they had won.

The vote was 2,670 to 821, a margin of three to one.

They had somehow triumphed over the moneyed interests.

They had saved their hillside.

They felt euphoric and empowered, and they resolved to parlay this ad hoc action into an organized, ongoing political movement, a powerful voice for the community. Emboldened by their first victory, they came up with a defiant and ambitious plan for repelling the wealthy invaders: They wanted to take over city hall in the November 2000 election.

If they succeeded, Sonoma might escape the fate of turning into the new Napa.

PART II

Interlude:

Napa

AT THE NAPA VALLEY Wine Auction of 2000, I discovered the fate that Sonoma's bohemians so desperately wanted to avoid.

It began with the man in black. No one knew who he was, but he was spending a spectacular amount of money.

He was dressed entirely in black even though it was an afternoon in early June and the temperature was in the nineties and he would remain outdoors for the length of the day. He wore a black cotton T-shirt and black dress slacks and black moccasins without socks. The stark attire suggested that he came from Hollywood or maybe Manhattan. His hair and goatee had a salt-and-pepper shading, and his skin was lined by the sun and the years, but he still looked lean and fit, which made it difficult to guess his age. He could have been in his early fifties or his middle sixties. He seemed oddly familiar to many strangers because he resembled James Coburn, the Hollywood actor who had been cast as Western gunslingers and military tough guys in early 1960s films with titles such as *The Magnificent Seven, Hell Is for Heroes,* and *The Great Escape.*

Even if he were the actor, the crowd wouldn't have been impressed. They were used to having celebrities among them. Bigger names had come here to the Napa Valley Wine Auction, the most important social event of the season in the most renowned wine region of America. Basketball great Michael Jordan had taken part in the previous year's auction. So had comedian Robin Williams, who owned a house in the mountains overlooking the valley. This time the event attracted Joe Montana, hall-of-fame quarterback from the San Francisco 49ers.

The man in black wasn't Coburn. No one among the wine cognoscenti seemed to know his name or his origins or the source of his wealth, which they figured must be extraordinary, given how much he was spending this afternoon.

Two thousand people had come, so many that the organizers had to erect the biggest tent that most people would ever see. The tightly stretched white canvas rose and fell in grand parabolic arcs, covering the first fairway of the golf course of the Meadowood resort and hotel. It sheltered a couple of hundred large circular tables. The center of each table had a metallic tub filled with ice and bottles of white and sparkling wines, and many bottles of fine red wines were arranged all around. With the plentiful alcohol and the heat, it was inevitable that most people would become pleasantly intoxicated. Any inhibitions that they might have had about spending large sums of money would lessen considerably.

If someone recognized the mysterious man in black, the intelligence would have passed through the crowd as people table-hopped and swapped bottles from the various vineyards with the eagerness of schoolchildren trading baseball cards during recess. But he didn't belong to their clubby circles. And he wasn't in the wine business. He hadn't been to the Napa Valley Wine Auction before. The other big collectors get to know each other at major auctions throughout the year at Christie's and Sotheby's in Los Angeles and

New York and London and Paris. And for the past three days they had seen one another throughout the Napa Valley at the series of food and wine tastings leading to this finale. They chatted as they left their Gulfstreams and Learjets behind at the Napa airport. They encountered one another while checking into their $2,000-a-night rooms at Meadowood and Auberge de Soleil. They visited one another's villas on the steep hillsides and splashed together in their lap pools and hot tubs and looked out at the dreamlike expanse of the valley below. Their Porsches and Mercedes and BMWs created drifts of fertile soil as they drove through the fallow field that served as a makeshift parking lot for the influx of auction buyers. They hobnobbed at the buoyant parties of the week, for which Napa's winemakers had brought in the most celebrated chefs from San Francisco, Los Angeles, New York, Chicago, and Las Vegas to prepare bountiful lunches below overarching trees at the edge of the vines and then extravagant black-tie dinners.

They hadn't met the man in black.

He remained silent for the first nine of the 166 lots that were slated to go up for sale. Then came Lot 10, the first of the so-called "cult wines," a ten-bottle set of cabernet sauvignon from Araujo Estate, with one bottle from each vintage year of the 1990s. Cult wines were a new and extraordinary phenomenon that inspired crazed passions among wine enthusiasts. They were small production runs from very small pieces of Napa Valley property reputed to have the most ideal climate, soil, and sun exposures, and they were crafted by a new breed of celebrity winemakers reputed to combine the artistic sensibility of the poet with the technocratic skill of a scientist. The critics proclaimed the greatness of these wines, confirmed by the clear authority of quantitative ratings in the high nineties or even the rare, perfect 100. Buyers struggled to acquire the vintages at whatever price. But cult wines couldn't be bought in stores: They could only be purchased directly from the vintner, which put the would-be buyer in a position of nearly hopeless supplication. You had to be on the winery's mailing list, but of course you couldn't get on the mailing list. It was a harsh exercise in frustration, denial, and inaccessibility that predictably created an extraordinary sense of aura, mystique, and unfulfilled longing. The rareness only fueled the determination and desire of wine buffs. There were skeptics, surely, but who could fairly denigrate a cult wine when so few people had tasted them? The lucky few touted the experience in nearly mystical terms because it enhanced their status as high priests of the cult. And just about the only way to enter the priesthood was to buy the wine at auction for conspicuously high prices.

The man in black raised his paddle and bid $270,000. The insiders turned and looked at him with astonishment. Two hundred and seventy thousand!

Who was he?

The first clues came from the members of the media. Several hundred reporters were covering the event. Their press packets included a list of the attendees arranged by the identifying numbers on their handheld white paddles, which they raised to make bids. The paddles signaled the hierarchy of power and prestige. Their numbering was determined by how much money the holder had spent at the previous year's auction. The biggest bidder won the honor of holding Paddle 1, the second-biggest bidder had Paddle 2, and so on.

The man in black carried Paddle 318.

He was . . . a *nobody*! An *unknown*!

The list said he was Chase Bailey from Incline Village, Nevada, a resort town on Lake Tahoe. It was one of those addresses that signified something very specific to people of a certain stratum. Many westerners were attracted to Lake Tahoe for the winter skiing, summer hiking, and the recreation on the big mountain lake. But an Incline Village address implied that the hidden motivation for being there was that the person made so much money that he needed a tax haven. The state line bisected Lake Tahoe from south to north, and Incline was the first waterfront hamlet on the Nevada side. Rich Californians could evade the Golden State's high income tax, which claimed nearly a tenth of one's earnings, by establishing residency just across the border in Nevada, that naughty holdout of freewheeling frontier laissez-faire where there wasn't any state income tax. In this way Incline Village is to Californians what Monaco is to Europeans.

So the man in black had some money. Still, it was rare for the auctioneer to see a six-figure bid from a paddle with a number in the hundreds. New players usually began much smaller and more tentatively. Bidding on the most expensive lots was typically dominated by the top two dozen returning bidders. This year the most impressive spending was expected from Dee Lincoln of Plano, Texas, a restaurant impresario who spent nearly a million dollars here the previous year and thus had the honor of returning as Paddle 1. She wanted to buy up the most highly esteemed and hard-to-get wines for her new Double Eagle steakhouse in New York's Rockefeller Center. She was rumored to have gambled $10 million building the 475-seat restaurant, and now she was spending prodigiously to stock its cellar. She needed trophy wines that her clientele could order for many thousands of dollars a bottle to celebrate their business triumphs. Her exuberant buying spree seemed calculated to bring her great visibility among the top connoisseurs and the publications that influenced them. Bidding a prodigious amount today at the auction was a key to her marketing strategy.

No one was surprised when she signaled her preeminence from the start by making the winning bid of $60,000 for Lot 1, a collection of sixty-six bottles, one each from sixty-six different Napa vineyards. Their expectations were fulfilled when she made the top bid of $28,000 to capture Lot 5, the four-course dinner party for thirty people at Merryvale Vineyards plus thirty-three bottles of wine. The meal would be created by the winery's own chef, whom it had lured from the legendary Alain Ducasse's Louis XV, a top-rated Michelin three-star restaurant in Monte Carlo.

"She's number one, man!" proclaimed the auctioneer.

But soon it turned out that she wasn't really number one. The man in black, Chase Bailey, had taken the early lead as the biggest spender, at least in this opening hour of the long hot afternoon, with his ante of $270,000.

A rumor finally circulated through the great white arched tent that Chase Bailey was an executive from Cisco Systems, which made computer networking equipment and at that moment had the highest stock market valuation of any company in all of capitalism. Its shares were worth a combined total of $500 billion, which made it more valuable than even Microsoft or General Electric. The crowd was knowledgeable about the stock market, yet it appeared no one had ever heard of Bailey. He wasn't one of the founders of Cisco, or the chief executive officer, or the chief technology officer, or any other leading figure whose name and photograph appeared occasionally in the press. He was an utter unknown.

For a while it seemed as though his spectacular bid would be his only one. The established players resumed their control. Lot 17 was a dozen bottles of wine blended by the quarterback Joe Montana (with a bit of help from a professional winemaker) plus a dinner for six with Montana himself. It sold for $210,000 to Paddle 14, a retired gentleman from the Napa Valley. Lot 25, a single oversized bottle of Colgin, another cult wine, went for $220,000 to Paddle 6, an heiress from Santa Barbara. The low-number paddles were prevailing again.

Lot 30 was eight bottles from a winery with an even greater aura, Dalla Valle Vineyards, and a lunch for six prepared by the chef Thomas Keller at the vintner Naoka Dalla Valle's hillside villa. Dalla Valle was one of the two or three most revered names among the short list of cult wines. Keller was the ultimate cult chef. Many critics had proclaimed that his French Laundry was the best restaurant not only in the Napa Valley but in America. It was much harder to get a reservation there than at any vaunted culinary shrine in New York or Paris. French Laundry only booked tables for exactly two months in advance of the day when the reservation was taken, but that rule was largely theoretical to most aspiring customers since it seemed utterly impossible to make contact with a reservationist. The place had a published phone number but the signal was always busy and no one ever seemed to answer it, even when desperate gourmands tried pressing redial buttons constantly on multiple phone lines throughout the day and evening. The concierges at Meadowood and Auberge du Soleil were rumored to have secret hotlines to the restaurant to secure tables for their guests, and that was a compelling amenity. But it meant spending an extra thousand bucks for a room as a prerequisite for spending a thousand bucks for a dinner. Besides which both inns are small and often booked maddeningly far in advance. San Franciscans began taking days off from work especially to drive an hour and a half to Napa and appear at the restaurant's front door in person and ask plaintively for reservations for two months hence.

As the auctioneer opened the bidding, Paddles 1, 2, and 3 were immediately thrust upward. Dee Lincoln triumphed with a bid of $270,000.

The biggest confrontation was still to come. Over the next two hours, as the auctioneer brought down the hammer on forty-eight more lots, the anticipation slowly built as everyone awaited the most sought-after prize of the afternoon.

The wine was called Screaming Eagle.

The vintner was offering just a single bottle.

"Screeeeee-ming Eagle!" shrieked the auctioneer into the microphone. His cry had a gleeful, piercing exuberance that he often had to repress during his regular gig at the podium at staid old Christie's in New York.

"Screeeeeeeeee!"

He opened the bidding at $10,000. Then, within seconds, the offers shot up into the six figures. There was great commotion as hundreds of people climbed onto their chairs and even onto the ta-

bles to try to get a clearer view of the big players seated in a cluster near the center. Cries and shouts resounded through the massive peaks and valleys of the high sweeping tent.

"*Five hundred thousand!*" screamed the auctioneer.

Then the gavel struck.

"That's the most expensive bottle of wine ever auctioned!" he
exclaimed.

The sound system blasted a recording of "Fly Like an Eagle" and
an entourage of cheerleaders ran out and formed a circle around the
high bidder:

It was Paddle 318. The man in black. Chase Bailey.

Nearby, at her own table, Dee Lincoln, who had expected to
claim the great prize, looked sad, shocked, and confused as she put
down Paddle 1.

"Who *is* Chase Bailey?" she said. "*Who is he?*"

Afterward, as he was accosted outside the great tent, he talked
politely but unrevealingly and he gave out his e-mail address to
journalists. It was chase@atleisure.net. He was a man of leisure. He
had indeed been at Cisco, but for only two years and his role there
seemed vague and he had already retired.

He spent $270,000 for the Araujo, $500,000 for the Screaming
Eagle, and $100,000 for dinner at the French Laundry with Doug
Shafer, a celebrated winemaker, and later in the day, near the end
of the auction, he paid $700,000 for ten bottles of red from Harlan
Estate. Seven hundred grand was the highest bid of the day for a
lot, but it was the half-million dollars for a *single bottle* that people
would remember and gossip about and openly marvel over.

The $500,000 bottle was the Napa Valley's apotheosis, the high
point of its ascendance as a symbol of status. It showed how far a
new-money type would go to seek entrance into Napa's exclusive
circles. In the coming months the $500,000 bottle would be de-
monized in Sonoma. It was a perfect element of propaganda for
Sonoma's populist revolt. The $500,000 bottle exacerbated the
people's resentment of the decadence and megalomania of the

elites. The $500,000 bottle was like Marie Antoinette saying "let them eat cake." The detail that ninety-five percent of the proceeds from the auction were donated to local charities—mostly to health care for farmworkers and the elderly—would be easily omitted, ignored, or forgotten.

And at that initial moment under the big white tent, before the news of the $500,000 bottle was circulated through the two valleys, even some of the assembled plutocrats found it outright astonishing. The price was more than the sum of the money spent in a week at an average supermarket by all of its shoppers. It was enough to buy eighty thousand bottles of wines that most people would consider good enough to serve at their own cocktail parties and dinner tables.

This last comparison is inexact because the $500,000 bottle of Screaming Eagle was unusually big: it was a so-called Imperial, containing six liters, making it eight times the size of the standard bottle, which holds only three-quarters of a liter. Even so, an eighth of the money figures out to $65,000 for a normal bottle's worth. And a bottle, however large, is still just a bottle. It's a risky way of storing such an expensive substance. With standard-sized bottles there is a small but significant chance that the cork will rot and ruin the wine, and the odds of contamination are even worse with oversized ones. Then there's the danger that a bottle might break during transportation or handling. And even the most astute owner might guess badly about how many years to wait before opening the bottle and consume wine that has aged a bit too long or not long enough.

Since a six-liter bottle pours out into thirty-six glassfuls, the $500,000 price represents about $15,000 for a glass. That meant that a single serving of the wine cost more than most American families spent on their apartment rents or home mortgages for a full year. A glassful costs almost as much as a new subcompact car; a single taste, a swirl, as much as a transcontinental first-class airline ticket.

And to make it all even more sublimely improbable, it turned out that Chase Bailey was a walk-in to the auction. He hadn't even signed up ahead of time to participate. He had the brazenness—or was it mere casualness?—simply to show up and barge in. The usual procedure for attending such an exclusive and expensive event, the polite and respectful way, was to reply promptly when the registration forms were faxed out several months in advance. The tickets cost $2,000 a couple and they typically sold out within three days of going on sale.

When Chase Bailey crashed the gates, the organizers were reluctant to let him in. They relented only after they made him commit to spend at least $10,000.

He single-handedly laid out a total of $1.7 million.

As I sat there and watched, I thought that if the revolution were to happen today, we'd be the first to die.

IN MY EFFORT to understand what was at stake in Sonoma, I was giving equal time to Napa. If that meant spending time in the enemy camp, no one back in Sonoma needed to know. So, on a typically warm, sunny spring day, I waited while Jean Phillips fussed. She was, perhaps naturally, nervous about serving what was reputedly the perfect wine.

We were seated in the expansive walled garden of the Tra Vigne restaurant in St. Helena, the prosperous little village at the center of the floor of the Napa Valley. The circular granite table was shaded by leafy overarching mulberry trees, and the walls were built from creamy bricks discolored to appear as if they had been naturally aged and weathered. The place instilled a sense of tranquility and sanctuary, and it seemed carefully calculated to feel like a Tuscan villa.

"When I want to go to Italy," she said, "I come to Tra Vigne."

When she first came to this restaurant, some twenty years earlier, the Napa Valley hadn't taken on its current aura and hadn't yet modeled itself on a romanticized conception of the Italian and French countrysides. This joint was called St. George then and it looked like a stuffy old men's club. But now it was a trattoria and it was extolled in the food and travel magazines from New York.

Jean opened her bag and showed me the Screaming Eagle label on a bottle. It was a conspiratorial gesture, as if she were a mischievous teenager revealing a plentiful stash of cocaine that she had somehow smuggled in and then flashing a sly smile to imply that we were going to consume it together and it was something that perhaps we shouldn't really do but it would be a lot of fun.

She had brought a bottle from her '97 vintage, which was supposedly even better than the '92 that Chase Bailey had paid so much for. This one, she said, had received a rating of 100 points from Robert Parker, Jr., the most influential of wine gurus. The flat-out perfect score was exceedingly rare. Not that she was motivated by the quantitative ratings as her ultimate goal.

"You make wine for your own satisfaction," she said. What was most important was that "you've tried your damnedest." And a top mark from Bob Parker or from James Laube at the *Wine Spectactor* was "icing on the cake."

But mentioning the perfect Parker review was playing a trump card. The great critic's opinion was so authoritative that it would probably inhibit many people from making their own judgments and maybe even daring to dissent.

Still, Jean seemed visibly nervous about having the wine tasted, understandably so, given all the hype, and she was careful to hedge.

The wine couldn't be evaluated fairly today.

It hadn't had time to breathe.

Her usual method was to uncork a bottle and decant it in the early morning so it could mix with the air for several hours before lunchtime. Then she would pour the wine back into the bottle and reinsert the cork just before she drove to the restaurant and hope the bottle didn't break along the way.

Letting the wine breathe for that long really did make it better to drink. It softened the taste and brought out the aromas. Even those who weren't wine buffs could appreciate a far more dramatic illustration of the same idea, which was taking a wedge of cheese out of the refrigerator and removing the plastic wrap and letting it rest for hours on the table until it was very smelly and soft. It made a difference. Still, a lot of people who considered themselves oenophiles and gourmands were always too harried or negligent for long, slow breathing.

This time, though, even Jean Phillips somehow forgot to uncork and decant, and the bottle was still unopened. So if I even tried to bad-mouth her wine, to say that it was a bunch of hype, I wouldn't be in a fair position to do so. For a moment I wondered whether this was her ploy for preventing dissent. I felt cheated, as though I were on a free weeklong trip to Paris and the weather stayed gray and rainy the entire time.

Still, I felt compelled to give her the benefit of the doubt. It was endearing that she was nervous about serving the perfect wine. And assuming that her forgetfulness was genuine, it would be understandable and easily forgivable because the fall harvest was approaching. Winemakers are always jittery until they know that the grapes have reached the ideal ripeness and it's time to pick and crush them.

"You're nervous until then," she said, "but there's no more fun than the day you start crushing. At the end of a hard day we have lots of music, beer, and tequila. And we have a bocce court. You can take the Mexican crew to the bocce court and instantly they're *Italian*. I take out a twenty-dollar bill and we bet. The Mexican workers don't like wine. *None* of them drink wine from the bucket at the end of the crush. Given the choice, they're going to take the beer or tequila."

As we shared her bottle, Jean reminisced about the auction.

"When they were bidding for Screaming Eagle, I literally had my head down and I thought that I was going to throw up," she said.

Her nervous lapses were appealingly humble for someone of such high celebrity within her own realm. She had recently been pictured solo on the cover of the *Wine Spectator* next to the headline: "The Rise of California's Cult Wines: Nine Superstars to Dream About." In the photo she looked quietly confident and deceptively youthful (more like forty than her actual age of fifty-four) and coolly attractive with her short, straight blonde hair and a slender figure in tight blue jeans and a clingy black top. She was the most talked-about and envied of the Napa Valley's several hundred vintners. And she was also a remarkably powerful real-estate broker. She was *the* person to see if you wanted to buy one of the best houses or residential sites or prime vineyards in the Napa Valley.

She was the ultimate insider in one of the most insidery of places.

Jean Phillips's wine was praised by the critics, but its aura as the number-one American wine—confirmed by the price at the summer auction, which set the pecking order for the coming year—was surely helped by the fact that she was the biggest player in the highest end of Napa real estate at a time when seemingly everyone with new money wanted to get in. And the reputation of the number-two wine, Harlan Estate, certainly had something to do with the fact that Bill Harlan was the developer and owner of Meadowood resort, which was where the wine elites loved to gather. And he was the man who created Tra Vigne. In some respects Napa was a shady little town run by a clique and the fix was always on.

In other ways, though, the Napa cult wines were a triumph of the free market. If the great wines of France and Italy evoked the feudal legacy of Old Europe—a vision of aristocratic families carrying forward centuries of tradition on ancestral lands and castles—then Screaming Eagle reflected the uniquely American character: It was shockingly new and it was made by a woman who came out of obscurity and invented herself through striving, opportunism, and hard work. Screaming Eagle was the rude capitalist retort to inbred nobility.

Jean Phillips was the daughter of a Baptist minister from Florida who left the church to become a real-estate broker. She wasn't an experienced winemaker when she came to the Napa Valley in the seventies. She was a small-time wholesale dressmaker. She took over an old factory space on Main Street in St. Helena and renamed it the Little Dress Factory. Then she began buying and remodeling other commercial buildings nearby. She took a three-day crash course in real estate and figured that she might as well get her broker's license, though she had watched her father struggle in that profession and had vowed not to follow him. But she did become a broker. In 1986, after six years of selling vineyards to other people, she listed a small ranch in the hills above the eastern edge of the valley.

"I had a flash: Why don't *I* buy it?" she recalled. It already was planted with some vines and it had a "funky old house" with a "killer view" of the valley floor and a very small barn—twelve by eighteen feet—where she could make her wine.

"I fully financed it. Like 110 percent. Then phylloxera hit"—an invasion of a tiny insect that infected the roots of vines—"and it killed every fucking thing. Wiped it all out." But a local bank rescued her and she persisted. "I've always been a dreamer and I've always had guts. I believe that anything is possible. In my bedroom I have a photograph of Amelia Earhart, who said: 'To experience the boon of living, you have to dare.' You have to be totally willing to fail."

In 1992 she picked grapes herself and concocted a homemade red wine in plastic trash cans and bottled it by hand. She burned a print run of labels when she thought that she would probably be the only person to drink it. As it turned out, that was the vintage that the *Wine Spectator* rated 96 out of 100, a shockingly high score from a publication that reserves even the low nineties for superlative wines. It was also the vintage that famously sold for a half-million dollars at the auction.

The way that Jean Phillips talked over lunch, she reminded me of two archetypes. The first image was that of the nonintellectual entrepreneur who repeats the sports metaphors and clichés popularized by too many self-help business books. When she handed over her business card, she made a conspicuous effort to point out that she had inscribed the motto of her winery, which was "Fly Proud, Fly Free," as if that were a clever phrase or a brilliant marketing ploy. Her earnestness was endearing, but a bit corny and unsophisticated for such an important player in the cosmopolitan culture of the very rich. She also seemed reminiscent of the lifestyle guru Martha Stewart, and the resemblance went well beyond the superficial similarity of their fair blonde looks. Jean Phillips was a determined do-it-yourselfer who bought a cheap fixer-upper and in a few years of hard work turned it into the new Château Margaux.

She had reinvigorated one of the most cherished collective fantasies of the overachieving members of the baby-boomer generation: their dream of early retirement. For many the vision was first inspired in 1990 by *A Year in Provence*, Peter Mayle's account of how he gave up his lucrative career as an advertising executive in New York and London to find an even more enviable lifestyle as he dined in good restaurants and enjoyed the sunshine while waiting for other people to come around and renovate the old country house he was living in.

Mayle's example appealed to the boomers' hedonism, but the chronic overachievers among them couldn't emulate his indolence and uselessness. They found a more appealing role model in Frances Mayes, a San Francisco poet and writing teacher who wrote *Under the Tuscan Sun*, about how she toiled on her superb cooking and gardening while she personally remodeled an old Italian farmhouse. She combined Mayle's passionate gourmandise with Martha Stewart's fiercely perfectionistic work ethic, and she could make others envy her achievements by describing them in lyrical prose.

Then Jean Phillips came along with her borrowed cash and she didn't even bother to renovate the funky old house. Instead, she made . . . the perfect wine! The 100 out of 100 points wine! The half-million-dollar wine! And she did it herself in that little barn. So what if Mayle could stomach a beef stew and Mayes could simmer a minestrone when Jean Phillips was rivaling Château Lafite in her own little backyard vineyard.

Jean Phillips personified the virtues of hands-on experience. "The world's conception of winemaking is ultimately romantic," she said, "but you can never really appreciate the wine until you've gotten down and dirty in the vineyard and you've gone through the whole process of making wine. You've got to love the wine business until your fingers are bright red." She talked about how much she'd like to work the harvest-time "crush" as a "cellar rat," a lowly manual laborer, at one of the big wineries in France or the Napa Valley.

Still, these days she hired a celebrated winemaker as a high-priced consultant to make Screaming Eagle for her, and she no longer picked the grapes herself. That work was so infamously hard that it was left for the Mexicans. But she still sorted the ripe grapes from the underripe and overripe ones by hand.

When I mentioned that I wanted to help work the harvest so I could have a firsthand sense of what it's like, she said: "You'll pick for about ten minutes. It's that hard." And when I added that I had heard from the Gallo people that Martha Stewart was going to pick grapes at their Sonoma vineyards for three days this fall, Jean Phillips was incredulous. Her skeptical look implied that the great icon of do-it-yourself wasn't tough enough to make it in wine country.

Jean Phillips represented the triumph of self-invention, and her example—trumpeted in slick magazines for wine enthusiasts—had a powerful influence on the new-money people who were coming to Napa. They overlooked the fact that she had lived there for a quarter century and made invaluable personal connections and was immersed in Napa culture for a long time before she tried to grow grapes and make wine. It was her seemingly instant stardom in the

Napa Valley that resonated with the entrepreneurs and executives who had achieved seemingly instant wealth and celebrity in Silicon Valley during the great boom of high-technology stocks on the NASDAQ market. It appealed to their own myth of having overthrown the old order in a few quick years through their supreme intelligence, long hours, and access to capital.

At that time a large-scale study at San Jose State University was examining the beliefs and aspirations of thousands of professionals who worked in Silicon Valley, and it found that their common fantasy was that once they made their killings they would move to the wine country, perhaps to own a vineyard or a charming country inn. The new elites desperately wanted to be Jean Phillips.

If one sign of sophistication was buying fine wine and being able to appreciate its many subtleties, then actually owning a superb vineyard meant even higher status, and personally making the wine conferred great prestige.

Napa held an extraordinary appeal for the technocrats, as it had for several waves of people before them who made their money in prosaic businesses and humdrum places and yearned for the elan of a glamorous pursuit in a beautiful setting, and as it would for the future waves of nouveaux riches.

The Napa Valley was becoming the new ideal of the moneyed class. It had the scenery of the country without the hardships and inconveniences and sacrifices. It was nature improved by human rationality, where the haphazard landscaping of the real country had been replaced by neat rows of green vines in rectangular blocks that appealed to the eye when seen from above, imposing a clean and artificial order on the unruly wilds.

"The vineyards are the world's most expensive landscaping. They're so *geometric*," said architect Olle Lundberg. "The land in Napa is stunningly beautiful. The valleys and the rolling hills—these sites are as good as you get."

The Napa Valley was much prettier than Bordeaux, which had some old castles but was dominated by a grimy industrial city. The food was as good in Napa as in Tuscany or Provence, and everyone spoke English.

Napa was even more exclusive than the Hamptons, with far fewer high-end properties. While the Hamptons had many miles of beachfront, Napa had few roads leading up through its foothills and mountains and few sites that commanded the spectacular views of the valley. And many of these rural lands couldn't supply enough running water or handle the septic needs of a modest cottage, let alone a hulking trophy house.

Napa had the best wines but you couldn't buy them; it had the nation's best restaurant but you couldn't get a reservation there; and many of its loveliest châteaux and vineyards weren't open to the six million tourists who drove through every year to taste wines and enjoy picnics.

There was an invisible velvet rope in the Napa Valley, and Jean Phillips could move it.

At the close of our lunch, I realized that the bottle was empty, and she had let me drink almost all the Screaming Eagle myself. I was in a very pleasant state, and she joked that it was lucky that I didn't have a few million dollars or otherwise she might have sold me a country house by the end of the afternoon.

ROBERT MONDAVI was in fine health as he neared his eighties. His vigor and enthusiasm made it easy to believe the ancient folk wisdom and the recent scientific evidence that drinking a couple of glasses of red wine every day improved health and longevity. But he was recovering from back surgery at the time of the Napa Valley Wine Auction in June 2000, and he often had to leave the scene in the big white tent to go lie down in his car in the parking lot. So he had to be a low-key presence at the event, which wasn't his inclination. He enjoyed the spotlight. At a previous year's auction he had even pretended to be a movie character as part of a humorous stunt to help incite the bidding. There was a ridiculous gizmo of a console that held a collection of wines—the kind of thing that might be found at a Sharper Image store—and the auction catalog described it as the "James Bond table." When the lot number was called, the table rose up dramatically through a hole in the stage, and there was Robert Mondavi in his tuxedo. "The name is Bond," he said with a straight face. "James Bond."

He was conspicuously short but he had always been athletic—he played football on his high school team and rugby as an undergraduate at Stanford University and now, six decades later, he swam laps in the long pool *inside* his enormous living room. He was leonine and handsome, and the passage of years and the remnants of white hair gave him a distinguished air that fit his public image as an elder statesman. In more private circles he was also known as a harmlessly dirty old man who would sweep his arm around the waist of a woman in her twenties, squeeze her tightly against him, and tell her with delight: "I'm so old that I can get away with this!"

Even with his back pain he was a trouper, so he put on his formal clothes again and showed up at the black-tie Vintner's Gala dinner under the white tent on the night before the auction bidding. The chef was his daughter-in-law, Holly Peterson Mondavi, who had trained at La Varenne, the famous cooking school in Paris, and now ran a specialty food business, Holly's Cooking Basics, which imported sun-dried preservative-free sea salts from France's Brittany coast.

Her cooking that night wasn't basic at all. It was hard enough to supervise the preparation and rapid service of any meal for two thousand people, let alone a five-course marathon for hypercritical gourmands. But she performed remarkably well. Her makeshift tent of a kitchen sent out great quantities of caviar on ice; chilled lobster with wasabi; lasagna of golden chanterelles, black trumpets, morels, and portobello mushrooms; and spring lamb with baby vegetables. And with it all there were great flows of wines matched to the flavors of each dish: sauvignon blancs and viogniers and pinot grigios and chardonnays and pinot noirs and cabernet sauvignons and merlots and zinfandels and meritages and moscatos and late-harvest dessert wines. The crowd was especially impressed with Holly's finale, a Meyer lemon mousse with cassis, because every plate was decorated painstakingly to resemble the wildly colorful glass sculptures by Dale Chihuly, a famed artist whose work was in the collections of many fine museums. Chihuly had created a series of monumental new works that were on display on the grounds beyond the big tent. They looked like giant penises in Day-Glo oranges and reds and purples.

I was about to voice this opinion when I realized that the sculptor himself, a portly man whose sloppy casual clothing stood out among the swells, was seated across from me at the head table. He was next to this year's chairperson of the auction, Nancy Andrus, the owner of the Pine Ridge winery.

"We're all *very* concerned about this book you're writing," she told me.

She seemed tough and intimidating. She was a tall, lean brunette, and her sleeveless black cocktail dress showed off her toned biceps and triceps. It was well-known that she had recently climbed to the summit of Mount Everest. I didn't have to ask Nancy Andrus why she and her friends were suspicious about an independent journalist snooping around their insular society. A decade earlier the writer James Conaway had published a dense historical account entitled *Napa*, and all the insiders still denigrated that book. They closed ranks because Conaway had described the flagrant extramarital affairs and embarrassingly eccentric behavior of the wife of John Daniels, the owner of Inglenook and the leading figure in the valley before the rise of Robert Mondavi. I never heard anyone suggest that the book was inaccurate, or that the material wasn't relevant and necessary for understanding the man's life and career. They were simply shocked that anyone would dare to write something unseemly about a member of their little club. They felt accustomed and entitled to public-relations puffery and the blithe hype of slick magazines that always idealized them.

Nancy Andrus was next to the woman who would carry Paddle 1, the steakhouse magnate Dee Lincoln, who was also tall, lean, brunette, and buff. She looked fortyish. I sat next to Dee's date, John from Dallas. There was much whispered debate throughout the week about whether John was her husband or her trophy boyfriend. While she was pretty and well dressed and had a southwestern charm, he was even prettier and even better dressed and his charm oozed while hers sluiced. He looked like the television actor Don Johnson after the pastel years of "Miami Vice" but before the middle-aged comeback effort of "Nash Bridges." He had the subversive smile and the deep tan and slick grooming of a highpriced gigolo in a Hollywood movie.

He gestured across the table to Dee Lincoln's financial backer, Jamie Coulter, the impresario of the Lone Star Steakhouses, a national chain with hundreds of relatively pedestrian restaurants, and then at Jamie's overtly sexy girlfriend.

"Her name is B.J.," John told me with the lascivious grin of a teenager.

Then John talked about the sex appeal of the women in Dallas.

"They all wear high heels like this"—he spread his index finger and thumb to their full extension—"and they wear skirts cut to here"—he pointed along the top of his own thigh almost to the point where it met the pelvic bone—"and let me tell you, I was happy to be a bachelor for a very long time."

NONE OF THE ELEMENTS of the scene that night—the atmosphere of opulence and excess, the fetishising of fine cuisine, the cultivation of famous artists and the commissioning of their works, the invasion of the new-money moguls—none of that could have happened there a generation earlier. The Napa Valley that existed in the popular imagination, the Napa Valley that had an aura and mystique, the Napa Valley that connoted sophistication and status, the brand name that represented the finest in wine, food, art, and lifestyle, was a recent creation, and it came about because of the vision of one man. The Napa Valley was invented by Robert Mondavi. Not the place itself but the conceptualization of the place, the image and identity. Many others came to share his quest, and their efforts contributed greatly to its ultimate triumph, as did Mondavi's own abundant charisma and brilliance and charm and energy. But Mondavi's inspiration was responsible for starting it all and sustaining it. The Napa Valley was the biggest tourist attraction in California after Disneyland, and it reflected Mondavi's vision almost as much as Disneyland represented Walt's vision.

It all began when Robert Mondavi had his midlife crisis.

The year was 1962, and the Napa Valley was strictly hicks in the sticks, an isolated rural enclave where the natives took a weird pride in their provincialism and backwardness. It wasn't wealthy or glamorous. It was the kind of place that history had flirted with and abandoned. Its great promise as a wine region was well-known when the Gold Rush brought an influx of people and money to northern California. By the late nineteenth century Napa had 166 wineries. Many were enchantingly rustic stone structures, and a few even aspired to the architectural grandeur of minor European châteaux. But the wine business was devastated by a massive outbreak of phylloxera around the turn of the century, and then it was beaten down by Prohibition. It remained down through the austerity of the Depression and the war years. When the federal government covered the nation with interstates in the fifties, the new freeways didn't come near the Napa Valley. Even though the valley's geographic center was only about seventy-five miles from San Francisco, the slow local roads put Napa a very safe distance from urban sprawl. It was protected from dense tract-house subdivisions and gargantuan indoor shopping malls and industrial parks.

Many of California's other farm regions were rapidly urbanizing. At the end of World War II, the Santa Clara Valley to the south of San Francisco was still a bucolic expanse of apricot, almond, and prune orchards, and local boosters promoted it without too much exaggeration as "the Valley of the Heart's Delight." Before long it was built up to become Silicon Valley. The San Fernando Valley to the north of Los Angeles, an idyllic land of orange groves, became a banal, smoggy suburbia, the classic example of what went wrong with postwar growth.

The Napa Valley wasn't much farther from an expanding metropolis, but it remained aloof. The one exception was the small city of Napa at the southern end of the valley. It survived as a bedroom community for workers who commuted to the military bases and shipyards at the northern shores of the bay. The town was working class and conservative with a strong redneck streak.

North of Napa city, the valley turned overwhelmingly rural. Cattle and horse ranches and prune and walnut orchards were as commonplace as vineyards. Thirty thousand acres of farmland spanned the two-mile-wide valley floor between the Mayacamas mountain range on the western side, which rose to twenty-eight hundred feet at Mount Vedeer, and the Vaca range on the eastern side, which reached its highest point at forty-five hundred feet at Mount St. Helena. A two-lane road lined with live oaks and eucalyptus ran thirty miles northward through the valley's center alongside the tracks of a defunct train line.

The road passed the sleepiest of towns. Yountville consisted of a state-run home for old veterans whose main pursuit was getting drunk at a string of bars and then loitering and hobbling on Washington Street. Then came Oakville and Rutherford, which might have looked like actual towns on the map but boasted little more than post offices, an old-fashioned country store, and an old grange. What passed for the gentry lived a bit further up in St. Helena, a pretty village that had retained its nineteenth-century Victorian character because there had been such scant economic development since then. St. Helena wasn't pretentious. It had a Main Street where a workingman could buy the clothing he needed.

The valley ended in Calistoga, which still had an Old West feel. The town's buildings were originally erected in the nearby mountains for silver miners extracting a motherlode. After they took all the metal, they moved the structures down to the valley floor.

Through the twentieth century the town survived off the city folks who came for its natural geothermal hot springs. The relatively small number of tourists to the Napa Valley drove right by the vineyards on the way to Calistoga for mud baths. In the late fifties, a vintner named Joe Heitz had the idea of putting a sign on the road inviting the motorists to come in and try samples of his wines. He invented the "tasting room." But back then most people kept driving in their fervor to see Calistoga's Old Faithful geyser.

In the early sixties, when Robert Mondavi had his transformative vision, there were only about two dozen wineries in the Napa Valley, and only a half-dozen of those even attempted to make quality wines. The vintners were typically Italian-American families with surnames that ended in vowels, and they made inexpensive jug wines for southern European transplants like themselves. For them wine was a daily consumable rather than an occasional luxury or a sign of sophistication or a vehicle for social climbing or a subject for scholarly debate.

Robert Mondavi's father, Cesare, was a poor Italian immigrant who built his Charles Krug Winery into one of the largest in the Napa Valley. But soon after Cesare died in 1959, Robert felt the family business was stifling him. In 1962, at the age of forty-nine, he traveled to Europe for the first time. He toured the great wineries of Tuscany, Burgundy, Bordeaux, and Germany's Moselle, and he dined at La Pyramide, a Michelin three-star restaurant in Lyon. The trip was a "revelation," he wrote in his memoir, *Harvest of Joy*. He was extraordinarily impressed by the elegance and refinement of the food and wine, which he described with terms such as "sophistication," "gentleness," "subtlety," "character," "balance," "harmony," "style," and "high art." And he conceived of re-creating the Napa Valley's wines and the place itself in the image of the European wine regions.

Back home Robert's grandiose ambitions were opposed by his older brother, Peter, a more modest fellow who ran the business with him.

Then came the legendary fur coat incident.

Robert and his wife, Marge, were among a number of Italian-Americans invited to a state dinner at the Kennedy White House to honor the prime minister of Italy. Marge despaired that she would look unfashionable to Jackie Kennedy, and she was especially concerned that she didn't have a good winter coat, an item that hadn't been necessary in the mild climate of the Napa Valley. The couple went to I. Magnin at San Francisco's Union Square and bought a mink coat for $2,500. The expense was a hardship, since Robert was earning $24,000 a year, but they vowed to stop going out to restaurants and movies.

To Peter Mondavi the episode showed Robert's excess of egotism. In 1965, Peter accused him of embezzling from the family business because that had to be the only way that he could have gotten the money for the infamous coat.

Robert punched Peter twice.

And then he left to start his own company.

His success came partly from making very good wines. Whenever I've asked Americans if they recalled the bottle they tried in their formative years that inspired them to learn more about wine and then pursue careers in the wine business, they were most likely to mention a vintage of Mondavi Reserve.

His effort to promote the Napa Valley's reputation as a region had its first triumph of international publicity in 1976, when the American bicentennial celebrations in Paris included a well-publicized blind tasting of French and American wines with a panel of vaunted experts, and the Napa vintages beat the best from Bordeaux and Burgundy. The results were more astonishing to the readers of newspapers than to the true insiders, who knew about the risky unpredictability of that kind of contest. Experiments at the University of California at Davis, where the viticulture and oenology program was reputedly the best in America and one of the world's best, revealed that even the top experts couldn't distinguish between red and white wine in blind tastings held under certain conditions. The phenomenon was called "Davis Syndrome," and it provided a snappy retort for any casual wine drinker who had to defend his own tastes from snobby criticism.

Nonetheless, the 1976 tasting created invaluable hype, and Robert Mondavi followed up on it with an equally brilliant marketing idea. He conceived of holding a wine auction modeled on the famous one held every year in Beaune, the market town in Burgundy. The proceeds would go to charity, but the real motivation was to promote the image of the Napa Valley and its wines.

The event had such a difficult start that even Jean Phillips, with her gregarious personality, had trouble giving away tickets to the first annual auction in 1981. The recession had affected even the plutocrats, and it was hard to attract wealthy out-of-towners when there still wasn't a good restaurant or a good place to stay.

During the great economic booms of the 1980s and 1990s, the foodie missionaries colonized Napa, the fancy inns opened, and the wine auction turned into a social scene. It became a way for rich people from other parts of the country to get to know the valley and to be enticed by the lifestyle and the aura of the wine business. It was a chance for the insiders of Napa's club and its aspiring members to meet each other. It was like open house at the best fraternity or sorority on campus at the start of rush season—everyone was checking everyone else out.

Charles Sawyer was the king of the propane business in Louisiana and Florida when he came to the wine auction in the mid-1980s. He liked the Napa Valley so much that he moved there. Jean Phillips sold him a ranch house and an old barn on fifty acres near the Mondavi winery. Then he hired a good winemaker and some other experienced hands from Mondavi. Early every morning he walked through his vineyards to look at the new crop. He loved it when people complimented his cabernets and his merlots. And he would respond: "You know, no one ever told me: 'Charlie, I really love that propane you make.' "

With each successive year Robert Mondavi's vision attracted

more and more of the Charlie Sawyers of America, people who bought into the dream. And it also appealed to people who already belonged to the glamorous international elite, such as the late Gustav Dalla Valle, who bought his land in Napa and moved there in 1982. Dalla Valle came from an old wine family in Italy. He had made his own reputation as the business partner of French undersea explorer Jacques Cousteau. In the 1970s he lived on a Caribbean island and was known as a great ladies' man. He married a young Japanese beauty named Naoko and took her to Napa to start a family. He died in 1995 at age seventy-eight one year before Naoko came out with her first vintage of red wine.

The French wine masters began their invasion of the Napa Valley in 1982 when the Rothschilds, proprietors of the great Château Mouton-Rothschilds, formed a joint venture with Robert Mondavi to create an expensive wine called Opus One. Their Bordeaux rivals from Château Petrus arrived the following year with the debut of their own Napa label, Dominus, which sounded haughtily like a Latin mispronunciation of "dominance" and signaled a new arrogance. The scion of the Petrus clan, Christian Moueix, declared that he was going to sleep outside on the ground of his Napa vineyard so he could gain a more instinctive feeling for the land. Then the locals told him about the profusion of rattlesnakes, and he decided to stay inside. Despite the culture shock, the arrival of the French (not only the princes of Bordeaux but also the lords of Champagne—Chandon, Mumm, Taittinger) secured Napa's new global status.

The worldly elite began building new wineries as conspicuous architectural statements. Sterling Vineyards carried tourists by a cable-hoisted tram up a three-hundred-foot knoll to a starkly white modernistic concrete structure that looked like a Greek island enclave crossed with a sprawling monastery. Jan and Mitsuko Shrem, owners of an international publishing empire, commissioned the San Francisco Museum of Modern Art to hold a competition for the design of their new winery, Clos Pegase. They wanted a showplace for their collection of twentieth-century abstract and surrealist art by Jean Dubuffet, Yves Tanguy, Joan Miró, Wassily Kandinsky, and other masters. The winner, Michael Graves, created a post-modern palace that the critics loved and the locals despised. The Shrems put a massive bronze sculpture of a thumb in front of their colorful hybrid of an Egyptian and Greek temple across the street from Sterling's Mediterranean fishing village.

But the clincher of the transformation was the Napa Valley Wine Train, the brainchild of Vincent DeDomenico, the magnate behind San Francisco's Rice-a-Roni. In 1986 he conceived of taking wealthy tourists on a restored train of luxurious Pullman dining and lounge cars—resplendent with mahogany, brass, etched glass, and expensive fabrics—that would stop at many wineries as it made its way for thirty-six miles on a three-hour trip over long-abandoned old railway tracks running up through the valley's center. Many of the locals thought the Wine Train marked Napa's crossover to tourist trap from working agricultural community. They fought DeDomenico politically for nearly four years before he was finally able to launch his service.

By the end of the nineties, the Napa Valley had been largely transformed. The city of Napa, also known as "down valley," was still embarrassingly white-trashy. But Washington Street in Yountville, where the drunken veterans used to carouse, was now the site of French Laundry and chef Thomas Keller's second restaurant, an informal brasserie called Bouchon, as well as Bistro Jeanty, which made *Gourmet* readers sigh with its image as the perfect country café. Tiny Yountville had more top-rated restaurants than many major cities. And it had spas that offered $100-an-hour massages and hotels with $700-a-night rooms. At dawn a dozen colorful hot air balloons carried visitors above the town.

The old-time general store farther north became the Oakville Grocery, and it still had a retro Coca-Cola advertisement painted on its exterior wall, but inside it was an emporium that astonished gourmands with its great variety of olive oils and vinegars and mustards. But its selection of food and wine was far eclipsed by the Dean & DeLuca that opened in a converted lumber warehouse. Normally it took a great affluent city like New York to support a store like Dean & DeLuca, but there it was in St. Helena, population five thousand. The storefront on St. Helena's main street that had once sold workingman's clothing was now a branch of Wilkes Bashford, one of the most expensive fashion boutiques in San Francisco, selling the finest Italian suits for thousands of dollars apiece.

The number of wineries had grown into the hundreds again, and many had tasting rooms, which were extraordinarily popular in the gilded Napa of the eighties and nineties. They had designs by famous architects, and they had art galleries and scenic places for picnics and they ran tours and held concerts. The film director Francis Ford Coppola's winery had a museum to himself, a one-man Planet Hollywood with props like Marlon Brando's desk from *The Godfather*. Napa had become an adult Disneyland for the affluent.

But the millions of people coming through every year might sense that there was another Napa Valley that they weren't invited to. The wineries that made the most expensive and revered vintages were not open to tourists. The houses on the hillsides could be glimpsed from a distance, but never visited. The public Napa had become impressive, but the private one was more spectacular.

NO ONE REPRESENTED the ideal of the good life in the Napa Valley better than Gil Nickel. He owned more than a dozen vintage luxury and sports cars—including multiple Bentleys, Ferraris, and Jaguars—and he drove them himself in competitions around the world. Every year he took a motorcycle trip through remote locales like Nepal on one of his nine BMW bikes. He flew in a private Learjet. He had a superb Italian chef who cooked on his yacht in Portofino. At home in Napa his personal French chef could rival any culinary star in the nation. He had restored one of the most historically important nineteenth-century wineries, Far Niente, and it was an especially beautiful place. He made cabernets that sold for more than $100 a bottle and sweet dessert wines that sold for as much as $100 a *half* bottle, and they brought him great prestige. He enjoyed a position in the Napa Valley's innermost circles. Gil Nickel and his wife, Beth, were so friendly with Jean Phillips that they went along when she *eloped* to Venice.

Gil Nickel threw the most elegant of the hundreds of parties during the Napa Valley Wine Auction. It was a black-tie dinner for 150 people. The stone facade of his old mansion of a winery was illuminated mysteriously with spotlights that revealed some features and left others obscured by the darkness. The guests walked down a gently curved stone stairway and over an arched footbridge to a little island that was covered by a sculptural halo of a white tent and surrounded by a serpentine pond and an enveloping sea of vineyards. Of course there was moonlight. The five courses were each prepared by different pedigreed chefs competing to outdo one another. The guests danced to a swing orchestra, and they consumed prodigious quantities of very expensive wine.

And in Gatsbyesque style, the host wasn't even there.

He was in Europe racing cars for the five-month season, and then he would cruise the Mediterranean in his boat before returning for the fall harvest.

Far Niente was Italian for "do nothing," and it was a beloved expression in Italy, where it was sometimes expanded to *dolce far niente*, or "the sweetness of doing nothing." But the Nickels did it all and they had it all. And it *was* sweet.

If Hollywood directors were casting the role of Gil Nickel, they would probably pick an actor with a commanding physical presence and an outsized personality that matched the character's exuberant lifestyle. But in person he was surprisingly unprepossessing. His manner was quiet and relaxed. His height was only average. Though somewhat broad and barrel-chested, he was not a big man. He had straight brown hair and a pleasant but unremarkable face, and around the winery he wore khakis and casual shirts with the company logo. He was hardly distinguishable from a winery hand. He looked like a prosperous Midwestern farmer, which is what he had been before he came to the Napa Valley.

He greeted me in the Great Hall of the Far Niente winery, where the row of oak tables was long enough to seat fifty for lunch. The building was on a knoll, and the Great Hall's windows looked high above the green valley floor toward the brown mountains. The winery was set a mile back from the valley's main thorough-fare, Route 29, and though millions of tourists could see it from afar, only Gil Nickel's friends and business associates were invited inside.

"The architect Hamden McIntyre designed thirty California wineries in the eighteen hundreds, including Inglenook, Trefethen, and Greystone, where the Culinary Institute of America is now," he said, "but Far Niente was his first one. When we bought it there wasn't a wooden door left in the building. The original corrugated tin roof had rusted and blown away. It took three times more time and money to restore than we had planned. The challenge was keeping the history and character of a hundred-year-old building without compromising the quality of our wines. We wanted Old World style and New World convenience."

Beth Nickel arrived and together they led me to his private of-fice. A signed handwritten note from Enzo Ferrari hung on the near wall next to a color photo of Gil driving a yellow Ferrari through the snakelike cliffside roads of Monaco in the late nineties. "I was leading that race until my brakes failed," he said.

A taxidermy of two pheasants and a partridge hung above the fireplace. "I bought that for two thousand dollars in Pueblo when my brother and I were riding motorcycles from the Mexico City Olympics to the Panama Canal."

An original bottle of Far Niente Sweet Muscat wine from 1886 was on display near his desk. "Let me dust it, honey," Beth said. She called him honey and he called her sugar, pronounced "shuh-guh."

He pointed out the line drawing on the bottle's label, which showed a hammock filled with grapes.

"The artist Winslow Homer was the nephew of the winery's founder," he said. "The label is unsigned but the Winslow Homer experts say it's his work."

The other wall-hanging was a black-and-white aerial photo of a large farm. "My father started a plant nursery in Oklahoma. We also have nurseries in Texas and North Carolina. Hundreds of acres. We sell to garden centers and chain stores. Twenty million plants a year. Twelve hundred employees."

He paused, then added: "I came here to get away from that."

He descended fourteen feet on a perilously narrow spiral staircase to the production floor below where the grapes were sorted and crushed and the large tanks held the fermenting juices. "Maybe if I'd noticed how many ladies came here in high heels," he said, "we wouldn't have done the spiral staircase."

Then he led the way into the caves, where thousands of French oak barrels of wine were aging in the naturally stable 58 to 60 degree Fahrenheit temperature.

The smell of wood was pervasive and heady.

"It's an underground city, that's right," Gil said. "Forty thousand square feet. We put in four hundred and fifty angles so it would be like a labyrinth."

He decided to excavate beneath the hillside in the early eighties. "I found a guy named Alf who built utility tunnels under streets. He used dynamite. I was scared to death. I made him put up a bond for more than the building was worth. He started out dynamiting a thousand square feet. The dynamite kicked up dirt and dust and small rocks, and the ground shook, but the building was fine. I said 'You're my man!' Those were the first wine caves in the U.S. since the Chinese laborers built them by hand in the nineteenth century. And now there's a three-year wait to build caves in Napa, and Alf is wealthy and famous."

A four-tiered chandelier with forty-two candles hung from the ceiling. It was custom-built by a sixth-generation Austrian craftsman. "I didn't want a chandelier for the top of the castle," Gil said. "I wanted one for the dungeon."

He led out of the caves and up to the "carriage house," a redwood barn that served as a private museum for his car collection. "When the bills came in I said that's too expensive to be a 'barn' so let's call it a carriage house." The dozen cars on display were only part of the full roster. "Unless some of my cars are out at the shop, I don't have room for them. I started buying old sportscars in the seventies and they turned out to be a big hit with our visitors, even if they didn't like wine. Some wineries have art collections. This is our mobile art collection."

There were Ferraris from 1951 and 1973 and 1990, black Bentleys from 1935 and 1953, a red Porsche from 1958, a red Corvette from 1961, a Miata from the early 1990s, a late-model Jaguar and two Jaguars from 1953 (a hardtop and a ragtop), and seven of his nine BMW motorcycles.

"Where's my London taxi?" said Beth.

These people owned so many cars that they seemed to have a hard time keeping track of them all.

A framed photo on the wall showed Gil in a bright yellow driver's jumpsuit. It was taken just after he won the European championship race for historic sportscars in 1995. "It was in the Czech Republic," he said. "They played the 'Star-Spangled Banner' and I felt like I had won the Olympics!"

A corner of the barn was filled with other collectibles and memorabilia. There was a Coca-Cola vending machine, boxing gloves from Muhammad Ali's trainer Angelo Dundee, and an old canoe as a reminder of when Gil won the Oklahoma canoe races.

It felt like the clubhouse of the world's luckiest boy.

A technician they referred to as the "dent guy" came by to inspect the cars. Gil went to get a worn old book that he called "the bible for Ferrari collectors." Its cover showed a yellow Ferrari from 1951. It was identical to the car that Gil was standing in front of. "It's the queen of my collection."

He led back to the winery, passing newly planted beds of lavender—"for a Mediterranean feel"—and olive trees that went back to the 1880s. The landscaping was as gorgeous as one might expect from the heir of a plant nursery empire. "We had twelve requests in one week to have weddings here," he said. "But I didn't want to become the Little Chapel of the West." The site was available only to employees and close friends. And of course it was where Gil and Beth had their own wedding after many years of living together.

When lunch was served under the gazebo, Gil began to tell his personal history in greater detail. "Growing up in the Bible Belt, wine is not part of the culture," he said. "I didn't taste any form of alcohol until I was thirty. My brother and I had a deal that we would alternate running the family business. I ran it for seven years, then handed it over. I wanted to get out of the way."

He moved to San Francisco, where he bought and restored a 1907 townhouse on Nob Hill. In the basement he found home winemaking equipment from the Prohibition era, when that pursuit had thrived. He began using it to make an amateur vintage and then audited classes about viticulture at the University of California at Davis. After searching the Napa Valley for three years, he bought Far Niente in 1979. The old winery had languished for a quarter-century, ever since the previous owner had died in a car crash.

During the three years they spent restoring the building, the Nickels lived like vagrants. "There were no good restaurants before Mustard's in 1983," Beth said. "There was no good place to stay. We bought a buddy's trailer for a bottle of bourbon and parked it by the trees. We called it 'Tara' as a joke."

"When we came here in the seventies," Gil said, "existing Napa Valley vineyards sold for six thousand dollars an acre while some vineyards in Burgundy and Bordeaux went for a hundred thousand an acre. And I said: If theirs are worth a hundred thousand, ours will be, too, because our climate is better. In the nineties I was the first guy to pay a hundred thousand dollars an acre for vineyard land in Napa. Now everyone with doggy land wants that price, and people think I got the deal of the decade. And now there are reports of a million dollars an acre for small vineyards in Europe."

After a four-course lunch of thin-crust wild mushroom pizzas, lobster salad with tomatoes and beets, grilled duck breast with peppercorn sauce, and blackberry vacherin, Beth showed photos from their yacht trip in Italy.

"Two farm kids from Oklahoma, there in Portofino!" she said with such gushing exuberance that it was surprising she didn't follow up with "Gee whiz!"

TWO WEEKS LATER, in late August 2001, the Nickels held one of their traditional Friday outdoor lunches for two dozen of their friends and associates. The harvest had begun the day before with the picking of chardonnay grapes, and Father Reginald from the nearby monastery had come to bless their ripe fruit.

"He's been blessing it every year since eighty-two," Gil said, "and every year has been a good harvest."

Gil was in a particularly buoyant mood since the previous weekend he had won a car race at the Laguna Seca track in Monterey, California.

"The kid is back!" he said.

The lunch was served on a long table beneath a row of thick-barked old trees. The trees resembled the live oaks that are common throughout northern California but actually they were cork trees, the kind that grow mainly in Portugal, where their barks are harvested to make corks for wine bottles.

"Cork trees take thirty-nine years until they generate their first cash flow," Gil said. "It takes thirty years until the first harvest, which you throw away. Then it's another nine years to the next harvest. Thirty-nine years. Can you imagine starting a business to-day if it was going to take thirty-nine years?"

Figuring backward from 2001, that thirty-nine years would re-verse time to 1962, when Robert Mondavi had his inspiration for reinventing the Napa Valley. In the time it would have taken to make a single cork, he remade the wine world.

I OWED MY CHANCE to live a bit of the good life in Napa to my friend Marc Benioff. Most days, Benioff lived in one of the world's most conspicuous locations for an expensive property: the top of Telegraph Hill. Nearly every one of the millions of people who came to San Francisco passed his driveway as they went a few yards farther to Coit Tower, the Art Deco monument from the 1930s. His modern three-story house of concrete and glass was virtually part of a famed tourist attraction. The views from the house's expansive east-facing windows were almost as spectacular as the views from the observation level of the tower, and much more private and privileged. He could step out on his deck and soak in his cedar hot tub and look across the water to the lights of the Bay Bridge.

Marc was thirty-five, and he had been at the top of the hill for a decade.

He was an executive at Oracle, the richest software company in Silicon Valley. He had started there right out of college at the University of Southern California. He began as a telemarketer, cold-calling potential customers. He learned that the secret to being a successful salesman was first to find out what the client really wanted, and then to figure out a way to claim that your product delivered exactly those features. If the client wanted software that was fast, your stuff was the fastest. If they wanted versatile, then nothing else was as versatile.

He was such a star as a salesman that he became the protégé of the company's founder, Larry Ellison, who was the second-richest man in the world in the 1990s. Larry elevated Marc to high positions in marketing and product development. By twenty-five Marc Benioff had the trophy house and the Porsches and the remarkable girlfriends. By twenty-seven he developed a precocious and profound ambivalence about his wealth and power, realizing that it wouldn't bring him lasting happiness and fulfillment. He began studying ideas from Eastern philosophies and religions, especially Tibetan Buddhism, and he sought a sense of balance in his life. He took six months off and established a charitable foundation and got a dog. But he never really gave up on money and power, or on real estate. He bought a vacation house in Hawaii's Kona, and later he purchased five acres of oceanfront property there on the Big Island, right next to the third hole of the golf course of the Mauna Kea Hotel. And in the late nineties, he spent $3.2 million for a house atop a mountain overlooking the Napa Valley, and he planned on spending millions more on a remodeling and expansion.

He wasn't the first person on to trends, but he had an instinct for getting in when things were about to take off: He had entered the software business in the eighties, and he had left his mentor and launched his own Internet startup in the nineties. He was a good proxy for what the Silicon Valley types would be thinking and doing. He reflected their culture and their unfulfilled aspirations. And he had great enthusiasm about trying to buy into the new dream in Napa.

But the people who passed for old money in the Napa Valley,

meaning the people who had been there since the 1970s, were divided over their attitudes toward the latest round of newcomers.
And the people who had struggled hardest to force their way into
the little club were among the ones who tried hardest to close the
door behind them. Napa's old money was really America's new
money, new enough to feel very threatened by the new new
money.

The problem was partly that the new new money was much
bigger than the old new money. Even though the old crowd had
bought in at six grand an acre and the wine business profited greatly
during the nineties' economic boom, their net worths still ended in
far fewer zeros than the new crowd's. And while the old crowd was
comfortable living in a farming region, the new crowd romanticized the country life but often had little idea of what it actually en-
tailed.

"It's going to be really interesting in the next few years," Beth
Nickel said. "We worry about the influx of nonagricultural people.
A lot of people buy homes and then realize there are farmworkers
and machines and they're spraying sulfur," a chemical that fights
mildew on the vines. The newcomers were easily irritated by the
loud noises of the great warming fans that rotate on late nights and
early mornings to prevent frost from damaging the grapes during
the crucial early weeks of the growing season. "In a few cases people have threatened the vineyards with lawsuits because the automatic propellers go off in springtime and it sounds like an aircraft
engine," Beth said. "But I like hearing them and knowing that my
little baby grapes are safe."

"This is a farming community," said Jean Phillips. "Even though
there aren't many people walking around in overalls, there is a
farming mentality. People worry about the weather. Farming is
what makes it a real, interesting place." Still, as a real-estate broker
she felt that people building big homes were good for the valley
since they provided stability during the periods when grape prices
were lower. The demand for expensive wine would rise and fall

with the economy, but a certain class of rich people would stay rich for a very long time.

"These new people have tons of dollars," she said, "and they're spending it differently than the Rockefellers did. The old money hoarded their money. But these people are making a huge infusion into the economy.

"In Napa I've seen people who have torn out their swimming pools and rebuilt them at ninety-degree angles. It's their choice. People have done very well. You should have things around you that are totally you."

That was precisely the way that Marc Benioff thought too.

MARC LIKED TO HOLD late-morning meetings at his favorite breakfast joint, Mama's, at the bottom of Telegraph Hill, across the street from Washington Square Park, where hundreds of elderly Chinese practiced T'ai Chi. It was a short walk from his house, but the difference in elevation was so sharp that he preferred to drive and hunt for parking. That was the unexpected drawback to having a fabulous view in San Francisco. When people first moved to the city, they were drawn inevitably to neighborhoods with names that ended in "hill" or "heights." That's what I had done, too. We spent our first few months enraptured: staring out the windows, watching tankers and sailboats cross under bridges, astonished that we were looking at clear water and sky and not the grime of a Manhattan airshaft. After a while, though, we got tired of having to sweat up our clothing and risk knee injury every time we went out for breakfast or coffee or groceries. So we joined the more practical longtime residents in the move to neighborhoods with names that ended in "valley" or "gulch" or "beach." If someone were living on a hill or in a heights after a decade, their desire to impress others was stronger than their yearning for convenience and community. Despite his long search for greater meaning, it seemed that Marc Benioff still needed to show off his success.

Still, I genuinely liked Marc for his warmth, intelligence, and humor. It was fascinating to experience his lifestyle voyeuristically. And I often thought that Marc represented what perhaps I could have been if I had made different choices. Our backgrounds were surprisingly similar: We were born days apart and we both grew up in comfortable suburbs with extraordinarily close-knit families, and we both advanced at precocious ages largely by replaying father-son relationships with powerful mentors. We were both fascinated by the hidden machinations of corporate power, which Marc experienced as an insider and I had struggled to uncover from the outside as an investigative journalist.

Now he was giving me the keys to his Napa house.

Marc arrived at Mama's wearing blue jeans and a baseball hat. He was a big guy, six-foot-five and broad-framed. With his dark hair and his sweet baby face, he looked like a nice Jewish boy who somehow grew up to be the size of a professional football player. As he entered the café, his presence boldly announced itself. He proceeded to greet almost everyone who worked at the restaurant by their first names and to catch up with Cyrus, the manager. He was a salesman by training, but he was genuinely interested in people. And even at a homey café, he liked to be known by all and to be treated especially well.

"In Napa, what I want is a sanctuary," he told me. "I want to build a private resort on the hill for my friends and family. I want it to be a service to my family and friends, the same way that they can use the Hawaii house whenever they want. When I build something I want to give, not take. I want to be of service.

"I have eighty-five acres, but almost all of it is part of the Napa County Land Trust. You can't develop any of it except for the small envelope around the house. It's about fifteen minutes up the hill from the Meadowood resort. You drive up a dirt road and then you come to a really beautiful place. The road is difficult to get up. It's dangerous. A truck turned over on it. We're going to have to clean up the road. But once you get way up there, the views are really incredible. Did you know that there's a lake hidden up in the mountains there? Lake Hennessey. From the site you can see Lake Hennessey and all of the Napa Valley. It feels like a very special, secluded place. A lot of people go to Napa for the social scene—the biking, wineries, tennis at Meadowood, lunch at Tra Vigne—and I'm going to do that too. But what I really want more is to sit on top of the hill and meditate. And I want to have my friends and family there."

He continued: "The house is fifty-five hundred square feet. The architect built it eight years ago for a gay couple from San Francisco who had a big collection of modern art. They made their art the focus of the architecture, not the view. The living room was designed around their huge Frankenthaler." And that was the biggest problem. There was a blank wall for a painting where there should have been a vast expanse of glass looking out on the wine country.

Marc wasn't a connoisseur of great art, but he was a collector of great views.

"I want to make the view the art," he said. "We will build a sanctuary on the hill. I'm putting together a world-class team. I've hired Michael Guthrie, the original architect. I've also hired Olle Lundberg, who was the architect of Larry Ellison's house in Pacific Heights. They're going to prepare competing designs. I've hired Donald Kaufman in New York. He's the most prestigious colorist in the world. He was hired by the Getty Museum for their walls. He mixes his own paints. Donald did the colors for my San Francisco and Hawaii houses. I've hired an interior designer. And I've hired the contractor in Napa who does everyone's houses up there, Tim McDonald. It's an extortion racket because the county is very controlling and he can get things through and the other contractors can't."

It sounded more like he was assembling an executive team for a company that would go public than remodeling a weekend place where he could sit in the sun.

A few days later he called his contractor for a meeting at his office. The headquarters of his venture, Salesforce.com, was in a high-rent Art Deco complex near the San Francisco waterfront. For a small startup the office was enormous—the open flowing space was a full block long and the ceiling was three stories high. Most of the cubicles and desks were still empty, presumably waiting for the dozens of new employees he planned to hire.

A very young and pretty female assistant in blue jeans escorted Tim McDonald into Marc's enclosed office. His glass exterior wall looked out on one of Apple Computer's "Think Different" advertisements, which plastered the side of a nearby building with a giant black-and-white photograph of Gandhi. The ledge of his windows was like his own tribute to famous political figures, or rather their tributes to him: There were separate framed photos of Marc next to Bill Clinton, Al Gore, Jesse Jackson, Benjamin Netanyahu, and the Dalai Lama. The display did more than simply give the impression that he had access to seemingly every world leader: It confirmed without doubt that he was taller than every world leader. There was also a photo of the dolphins that he liked to swim with when he spent time at his house in Hawaii. The inner wall of the office was covered with framed press clippings about him and his company's successes. His desk held an Apple computer and a very large, expensive flat monitor.

The men sat around a table on two of the office's six ergonomic Aeron chairs, which looked very high-tech and cost about a thousand dollars each.

Marc was wearing a vibrantly colored short-sleeved Hawaiian shirt.

"Fridays are aloha day here," he said.

Tim was dressed neatly in beige pants and a sports shirt with the top two buttons open. He was in his forties, a rugged outdoorsy type with a warmly handsome face and an enviable amount of thick brown hair. He looked like the actor Michael Landon did on "Little House on the Prairie" in the seventies.

Marc began the meeting by talking about what he liked the least about the Napa house's original design, the features he had asked his architects to rebuild. The gay men had put in a long narrow lap pool, but Marc didn't have any interest in keeping it. "A pool without a heater—in Napa?" he said. On a mountaintop, at more than twenty-five hundred feet, the evening temperatures were brisk even in summer. "Who are these people, part of the Polar Bear Club?"

Marc said that the gay couple sold the house a few years ago to some old fogy who was enamored of the decorating style of nineteenth-century British men's clubs. He remodeled the downstairs into a stuffy library with dark wood paneling and leather armchairs and oil paintings of old clipper ships. There in a natural paradise, amid the trees and lakes and mountains and all that extraordinary light, he wanted something so dark and stifling and phony! Tim, of course, was the contractor who helped the fogy to realize his vision.

"We did that funky library," Tim said. "And we'd be glad to tear it out."

"We can demo it," Marc said, meaning "demolish."

"The hardest thing we're going to have to do," Tim said, switching topics, "is pulling out the structural wall where the Frankenthaler was hanging."

"When we take out the wall, Tim is going to have to build a steel cage or a box to hold the house," Marc told me excitedly, like a boy playing with erector sets. "He's going to have to hitch steel beams on a helicopter and fly them in."

Marc reached for a long roll of blueprint paper and unfurled it on the table to reveal the proposed redesign from the original architect, Michael Guthrie.

"Michael wants to open up the kitchen," Marc said, pointing to the plans. "I really like this two-level deck he's designed. I like his idea of an outdoor fireplace. Michael has put a bedroom in the pool house, but there's no view from the bedroom. I told him, 'Michael, you've got to be kidding! We're building a pool house because we want the *view* from the pool house!' "

Marc unrolled another set of plans, this time from Larry Ellison's architect, Olle Lundberg. "I don't think that Olle is interested in the main house, frankly," Marc said, shrugging disappointedly. "He's like, 'This is Michael's house.' "

They agreed that the only thing that Olle seemed enthused about adding to the main house was a reflecting pool with water cascading down from an I-beam.

Marc liked the idea.

"For the last ten years Olle's been trying to sell one of these to his clients," Tim said. "But no one would pay for it. Until Marc."

What really excited Olle was the chance to design a spectacular pool house, which would be purely his own creation rather than a reworking of another architect's efforts. He envisioned an "infinity pool," where the water looked as though it was falling off a cliff, like a manmade waterfall. His plans showed a pool house with a loft bedroom and an indoor-outdoor fireplace—the two sides were separated by a translucent glass wall—and a hot tub built into the hillside. The surface of the entire pool area was covered with a prodigious amount of flagstone.

"This I think is really quite lovely," Marc said. "Olle wants to do it, you can see that. He even built me a model. And Michael wants the main house."

Marc pivoted and looked straight at Tim. "My problem," he said, "and the reason you're here, is this: How hard is it going to be to hire both of them? And can I delegate managing the two architects to you?"

Tim said that he was willing to take on the challenge.

"This way they both win," Marc said. "They both get photos that they can put in their portfolios." Marc was used to handling people with enormous egos. He had spent a full decade as the young protégé of a decabillionaire.

The discussion turned to finer points of contracting. Marc wanted Tim to make sure that there were no chemicals in the hot tub or the pool.

"A sauna near the pool is nice," Tim suggested.

"I like eucalyptus steam. Can you do eucalyptus steam?"

Tim nodded.

"Okay," Marc said. "And your wife is going to look at the doors, right?" He turned to me and explained in an aside: "Tim's wife is a feng shui expert."

"We'll need a pathway and a golf cart to get your parents to the tennis court," Tim said. "That will probably be a three-hundred-yard trip, and it's uphill." Marc agreed to the notion.

"And we might want a temporary gate during the construction," Tim continued. "Kids ride their bikes up there."

"If they can get all the way up there, then God bless them!" was Marc's response.

THE MAN HELPING the tech moguls realize their Napa fantasies had an office in a century-old stone building. It was in St. Helena, the prettiest of the Napa villages. There were a profusion of roses and white picket fences and trellises covered with flora and old palm trees. The town spread for only a few blocks before the landscape turned to vineyards and a few country mansions. There was no precinct for the working classes or for the immigrant and migrant farmhands. The small-town perfection of St. Helena was preserved for only the affluent. Others were banished to the contemporary ugliness of the city of Napa, which was comfortably far away beyond a vast protective greenbelt of vines. The Napa Valley was shockingly segregated.

Tim McDonald grew up in St. Helena before the gilded era. When he was a kid, his friends would hang out in the cellars at wineries and steal bottles and bang them against oak trees to get them open. He went away to college on a pole-vaulting scholarship, majored in "ag business," then returned home to work as a carpenter and live in a tiny cottage surrounded by vineyards. Now he found himself building extraordinary structures for the world's top architects.

The interior of his office had exposed steel beams that reinforced the rough stone walls and held them steady during earthquakes. He looked over a large table covered with blueprints for the Napa house he was building for Richard and Pamela Kramlich, a couple whose main residence was in San Francisco's *beau quartier*, Pacific Heights. Dick was a prominent venture capitalist, a veteran investor who made a great fortune by bankrolling technology start-ups for the past two decades. The Kramlichs already owned a week-end retreat in the Napa Valley, but they wanted a new space specially designed to display their famous collection of digital art, some of which would soon appear as a freestanding exhibition at San Francisco's Museum of Modern Art, where they were major benefactors. They also wanted their new house to be an artistic statement in its own right. So they hired the architectural firm that was working on an impressive building renovation for the modern art collection of the Tate Gallery in London. For the Napa commission the architects designed a seven-thousand-square-foot living space with walls of curved glass. For the Kramlichs' artworks, which need large spaces for the projection of electronic images, they planned a huge basement.

Tim talked about the construction challenges of realizing the architect's grand visions.

"The design is all glass," he said. "Dual-glazed bent glass. That's very difficult. It was hard to find people to do it for us. And the county had energy issues because it's all glass. So we're using radiant heating and cooling. And look at the roof. It's a free-form sculptural design with peaks and valleys. It's called a 'tension-fabric' roof: You can walk on it like a trampoline! There are only three companies in the world that can build this kind of roof, and they're in New York, Germany, and Australia. There are two pools: One is a lap pool and the other is an 'architectural element.' We're getting stainless steel from Switzerland for the pools. They're building it in pieces there. And in Germany we found a retractable pool cover that comes out over the middle of the water and then spreads out."

We got in Tim's pickup truck to go on a site tour, and he drove a few miles south through the center of the valley floor. Near the Robert Mondavi winery with its faux Spanish Mission belltower and arch, so familiar from the drawing on the labels of millions of wine bottles, he cut west to the foothills of the Mayacamas Mountains and arrived at the Kramlich site. He reached for his hardhat and walked over toward the top of a massive hole in the hillside.

The site was stunning. It looked like the excavation for a Manhattan skyscraper, not a hole for the foundation and basement of a weekend house.

Tim led along the scaffolding and down a perilous ladder to the bottom of the hole. The slab floor was already in place, and it looked large enough for a convention hall. "The art gallery is about a hundred and sixty feet long and fifty feet wide. Then there's another forty feet for underground parking. It's twenty-six feet high from floor to floor. The actual ceiling is twenty-four feet."

Retaining walls were holding back great masses of earth while the men erected the steel frames and prepared to pour concrete for the vertical walls.

"Once these walls are formed," Tim said, "I'm going to bring a couple of hoops and we'll play some basketball and have a barbecue."

He smiled.

"We're going to have to bring in some big structural steel by helicopter," he continued. "The helicopters pick up the steel from below, by the vineyards. The copters don't have to land at either point. They can do the roundtrip in three minutes, and we can set twenty pieces of steel in only an hour."

A pickup truck from Artistic Lighting was parked at the site.

The electrical subcontractors were involved so early in the construction because "the house will be controlled by touch screens connected to servers. They've already figured out where the electrical lines go to move the drapes."

Slowly we climbed back out of the hole. A wall of trees was blocking the multimillion-dollar view of the vineyards and the Vaca Mountains.

"We'll do a selective trimming of the trees," Tim said, "so you can see the valley floor from the 'entertaining area.' We have a landscape designer, Molly Chappellet, and she tells us which trees we can take away and which ones we have to leave. Her family has been in the wine business here for thirty years."

Tim drove his pickup up the hill to a small wooden chalet that served as the project contractor's office. The rustic house had an octagonal floorplan with rooflines sloping upward from the periphery toward the high anchor of a fireplace in the center of the flowing space. It was surrounded by lush trees, a deck, and a little pool, all overlooking the hillsides and the vineyards. This, I thought to myself, was the perfect rural retreat. It had a human scale and it blended so harmoniously with the natural surroundings. I'd rather live in the chalet than in the gargantuan structure they were building below. But to the owners it was just an overlooked remnant that happened to come with the land.

Tim introduced me to his associate Dan, who was going over plans.

"You could rent this place out on weekends," I said very enthusiastically, blatantly signaling my hope that they would offer to let me stay there once in a while.

"It's rented," Dan said a bit defensively, but then he eased up and even gave a sly wink. It was obvious that he stayed there himself on the weekends.

Tim pointed to a computer screen that displayed the website that everyone involved in the project used to share information in-

stantly, without having to wait for detailed plans and drawings to arrive by overnight mail deliveries. "There's a webcam out there on
a tree," he said. "The architect lives in Switzerland, and from his
computer he can direct this webcam to tilt and zoom and get real-
time pictures of the site. A three-hundred-sixty-degree panorama."

Imagine the contractor's client, the venture capitalist, sitting at
his office on the fifty-somethingth story of a skyscraper in San Francisco's financial district, looking majestically over the bay toward
the Napa Valley on the horizon, feeling as powerful as a modern-
day Zeus atop his Olympus. Then he would sit at his computer to
view his construction site via the webcam. He would be eager to
see his dream taking form in steel and concrete. Fiber-optic connections moved electrons at the speed of light and brought the images to his screen, but what was this? The men weren't working
diligently. They were playing a game of five-on-five basketball
while their foreman flipped fat burgers on the barbecue. This was
what digital technology made possible for the billionaire.

We got back into Tim's pickup and continued our tour of the
valley. A casual glance didn't reveal any other gargantuan trophy
houses in the foothills and mountainsides. A closer look would find
a roofline here and there, but the villas were spread out sparsely.
They didn't distract the eye from the natural scene. It seemed remarkable that such desirable real estate hadn't been covered with
houses and made to resemble the Hollywood Hills or the French
Riviera.

"In Napa today, you can't subdivide your property into anything
less than parcels of one hundred and sixty acres each," Tim explained. "So if you want to split your property into two pieces, you
need three hundred and twenty acres. That means that these hills
are 'beachfront property.' There are a lot of teardowns. There's
pretty strong opposition to development in the valley."

Tim steered his truck through the vineyards of the Staglin family, who were also his contracting clients. Garren Staglin, like Dick

Kramlich, amassed his fortune as a venture capitalist investing in technology startups. Lately he had been making some of the most talked-about wines in the Napa Valley.

Garren was the son of an immigrant from Calabria in the boot of Italy. The family's name was Stagliano before they removed two of the four vowels. Garren inherited a forceful nostalgia for the land. He didn't handle the farming himself, though. His vineyards were run by the same Napa native who oversaw the grape-growing for the other "cult wines" of the moment: Screaming Eagle, Harlan Estate, Araujo Estate, and Colgin. In the land of celebrity chefs and celebrity winemakers, even the farmers were beginning to take on cult status.

Garren and his wife, Shari, lived on a hill overlooking their vineyards in a ten-thousand-square-foot Palladian estate. Their walls were hung with museum-quality works by Chuck Close and other contemporary artists. The house had been featured in photo spreads in several slick-paged lifestyle magazines. Disney rented it out as the main location for shooting the movie *The Parent Trap*.

They had invited their neighbor Bob Mondavi to the groundbreaking ceremony for the house. Mondavi looked eastward across the valley and said that the lineup of architectural treasures reminded him of the great vistas of Washington, D.C. In his imagination the Staglin house was like the Capitol, the Mondavi winery was the Washington Monument, the reservoir for irrigating the vineyards was the Reflecting Pool, and the Opus One winery (a joint venture between Mondavi and France's Baron de Rothschild) was the Lincoln Memorial.

Garren Staglin had an equally grand conception of the Napa Valley's global significance and their own role in history. He said that families should serve as guardians and caretakers of the land rather than ceding it to companies whose investors clamored for short-term profits. He hoped that Napa would give rise to dynasties, and he spoke admiringly of the "generational patience" of Italian clans such as the Frescabaldis, who had been in the wine business for thirty generations over eight hundred years, and the Antinoris, who had lasted six hundred years.

The Staglins shared the Mondavis' passion for matching wine with food. Their organic gardens grew figs, strawberries, squash, tomatoes, and roses, all of remarkable size. They made olive oil from the fruit of their own trees. They could seat twenty around their outdoor "harvest table" made of granite from South Dakota, where Shari had grown up on a farm. The table was covered by a trellis with wild grapevines. Thomas Keller from French Laundry had cooked for them in their huge kitchen, as had the famous Charlie Trotter from Chicago and some of the most renowned chefs from San Francisco and Los Angeles. Shari liked to hike in the mountains behind the house with their neighbor Ellie Coppola, Francis's wife, until they reached Robin Williams's house atop Mount Vedeer.

The Staglins almost had it all, but first they needed caves like the Nickels had.

TIM MCDONALD PARKED at a construction site. There was a gash, twenty feet wide, in the side of the hill. It was the entrance to the massive caves he was building for the Staglins, where they would store and age twelve hundred barrels of wine.

He pointed toward a nearby house.

"The Cakebreads live next door," he said. The Cakebreads were a long-established winemaking family in Napa, and they were adamantly opposed to the Staglins' caves. "They said that this is a 'residential area,' even though they just put up a new winery build-ing of their own nearby. In Napa there are a lot of people who think 'We're in, now let's close the door behind us.' "

He drove past a huge pile of dirt taken from the Kramlich ex-cavation, which they were paying one of the neighbors to store for them. Tim would eventually need the dirt to cover up part of the crater he had put into the earth.

He steered by the Mondavi winery, where a huge, hulking, new winemaking facility recently shot up behind the original lower-rise structures.

"The Mondavis added two feet to the elevation of one of their vineyards with dirt from the excavation for their building expansion," Tim said. "Robert Mondavi's own house is near here. It has ten thousand square feet but only one bedroom."

He gestured toward the mountains to the east, where he was building a villa with hillside vineyards and a winery for a software entrepreneur from New York. The tech guys had become his most fervent clients. That afternoon he would go to the city to meet with yet another venture capitalist, who wanted to convince the county to let him build on an acreage that's preserved as part of Napa's Land Trust. And recently Tim sent a solicitation to every one of the fifty people listed by *Vanity Fair* magazine as the top players in the Internet business.

The next destination was Marc Benioff's house. The pickup bumped its way up the treacherous mountain road, passing a wild turkey from the large flock that lived there. Much of the mountain was once a single ranch belonging to a local woman named Mabel, who still lived there but had sold off large pieces. Her neighbor was Kevin Wells, the son of the late Frank Wells, a top executive and heir apparent at Disney who died in a helicopter crash. Kevin still traveled by helicopter to his eighteen-hundred-acre estate, undeterred by his father's death.

"The helicopter must make Mabel go through the roof," Tim said. "She has a reputation for being a little difficult."

"A few years ago I looked at buying Marc's site," he said as the road got even bumpier. "But I didn't buy it because I figured that all the infrastructure would cost around three hundred thousand—fixing the road, the water, the septic, the power. Now it's going to cost Marc four times that much."

We arrived at a sprawling concrete structure with the faded orange tones that made Americans think wistfully of Tuscany. The rooms were spacious and the house was in excellent condition throughout. It was a relatively new house, only eight years old and carefully constructed. Marc's remodeling was strictly a matter of putting his own mark on the property.

The downstairs was the dark Old English library that Tim was going to tear apart. The lighting fixtures resembled ram's horns, and they were indeed lacking in taste. But the library led into an attractively designed wine cellar.

"Marc wanted to remove the wine cellar!" Tim said. "Marc isn't really interested in wine. I told him, 'Marc, you *have* to keep it. This is *Napa*!'"

Tim led to the master bedroom. The views were superlative. It was the inner sanctum of what would be the bachelor pad to end all bachelor pads.

Tim broke into a slow, sly smile.

"You could have some great sex here," he said.

THE MOST FAMOUS RESTAURANT in the Napa Valley was the French Laundry, but the favorite among the locals was Bistro Don Giovanni. French Laundry was too formal: it was perhaps the last public place in northern California that still required men to wear jackets, even at lunch. Its reservations policy was impossible and the menu largely inscrutable: it relied on terminology such as "paquet," "brunoise," "hyku," "chibouste," "tomme," and "mignardise." The tasting menu had portions so small that they seemed like finger foods that waiters would carry on trays at cocktail parties rather than full courses at sit-down meals. The dining experience felt more like an exercise in literary and aesthetic showmanship than chowhound indulgence. The guest was supposed to marvel over the wit of the menu items' nomenclature during the long pauses between consuming the bite-and-a-half serving from each course during the three-hour marathon. One of the most famous dishes was called "Oysters and Pearls," a sabayon of pearl tapioca with poached oysters. Its weight could be measured more accurately in grams than ounces. Such was the supposed literary thrill. The visual pleasure was more palpable, since the chef's talents for precision and miniaturization were indeed impressive. But French Laundry wasn't a place you would fantasize about while hungry. And it was fearsomely expensive.

Bistro Don Giovanni, in contrast, was casual and boisterous and felt like being at a party. Even if the tables were fully booked, the hosts somehow found room for locals and regulars. The menu made sense to anyone who spoke Menu Italian, which was a second language for city dwellers in places like San Francisco and New York that had scores of decent trattorias. There were salads and pastas and pizzas and risottos and meats and everything was flavorful and bountiful.

Bistro Don Giovanni was so popular that the Napa Valley's citizens let it encroach onto their sacred farmland. There were thirty thousand acres on the valley floor outside the borders of the few small towns but most of it was untouchable. In 1968 the county put the farmlands as well as the hillsides into an agricultural preserve. It was all zoned for agriculture, and you could put up a farmhouse or a barn or a winery, but that was about all. Even then, the county wouldn't allow anyone to build on lots smaller than twenty acres. The minimum size was expanded to forty acres in the late seventies. Those shrewd requirements were what protected Napa from suburban sprawl in the seventies, eighties, and nineties just as its remoteness from the freeways had saved it in the fifties and sixties.

When the bistro tried to construct a patio so its patrons could sip wine while looking over the vineyards, it needed to encroach on the ag preserve and that required putting the matter on the ballot for the voters of the entire county. They said yes to the patio, but they surely wouldn't say yes to new houses. And so the real-estate market in the Napa Valley was driven by extreme scarcity. French Laundry's patrons could afford to live there, but others couldn't. By the late nineties the situation was so desperate that the

Bistro Don Giovanni habitués—the winemakers and the marketing people at the wineries and the local doctors and lawyers—began buying homes down valley in Napa city. They found themselves alongside a new wave of outsiders moving in from San Francisco and Silicon Valley: the unhinged technocratic professionals with kids.

John and April Stallcup represented the new immigrants to Napa city. John was almost fifty but he remained fit from frequent bicycling through the valley. He had thinning brown hair and a neat mustache. He wore the white baby boomer's uniform of khakis and a polo shirt. He looked exactly like what he was: a former corporate executive who had taken to his new life as a consultant working from home and playing with his small children. He first came to the Napa Valley several years earlier to work for Crystal Geyser, the mineral water company, and then became a marketing honcho for one of the big wine conglomerates. Now he advised about brands for technology startups.

April was a strikingly attractive black woman. She dressed like a fashion model's conception of a business executive. She presented herself with the buoyant self-confidence of a girl who grew up poor, left home at sixteen, and achieved her own success. Now she was an engineering manager who ran the computer center for a sizable company.

John worked from a desk in his living room. He needed to drive to San Francisco once or twice a week but only at offpeak hours. The couple stayed in Napa because they were able to buy a spacious high-ceilinged house in a bucolic neighborhood for one-third the money it would have cost them in other towns in the Bay Area. Their enclave was filled by what the author David Brooks had labeled "Bobos," for "bourgeois bohemians," the new class that fused the careerism and materialism of yuppies with a liberal idealism inspired by the counterculture. Their crowd wanted to transform the city of Napa into a "latte town." They were early gentrifiers challenging the defiantly backward culture of a place where the locals were passionately resistant to any kind of change.

"Napa natives call themselves Napkins," April said during lunch at Bistro Don Giovanni. "They hate *everybody*. They don't want anyone to move here."

"This town is a hundred years behind," John said.

"When we were going over the escrow papers, the real-estate agent said, 'You know, there are very few blacks here, or Asians, or Latinos.' "

"It's a classic Southern redneck town."

"I've lived all over," April said, "and this is the only place where I've been pulled over for being black. I was coming home at two in the morning after working late on a project. I drive a two-year-old SUV with a kid's seat, and the cop asked me if I stole it! I filed a complaint so I'll have a paper trail."

"Yeah," John said, looking at her affectionately. "I want to be able to sue someone if they shoot you when you reach for the cell phone."

"Now I carry a card with my congressman's phone numbers."

"In Sonoma there was a black guy whose kid left a toy gun on the backseat of the car. They took him out of his house in handcuffs."

"I was at my snooty gym," April said, "when the paper had a front-page story about three white kids with sticks chasing after three black kids. When I talked about it, people walked away. They didn't want to talk about it in public."

"One of these days, Oprah will get pulled over. Then things will change!"

"A big percentage of the local people have never left this valley. That's it, they've never gone anywhere else. They haven't *flown* anywhere. They've lived here their whole lives and they remember the whole history of things that have changed: when the dirt roads were paved, and when the first car dealership came in. They're very resentful about change. The Napkins were born and raised here and they'll never leave. The natives have pride that they are *n*th-generation and their mom and aunt live nearby and they have a boat on Lake Berryessa. Have you been to Lake Berryessa? It's a party lake. A lot of rednecks with long hair and tattoos. You know, people never used to think of Napa as 'exclusive.' Napa was the old mobile-home park where you put your grandmother. But in the last two or three years there's been a big influx of people from elsewhere. They live here and commute to San Francisco. It's really changing Napa."

"You've got a collision coming," John said, savoring the prospect. "The influx of highly educated people versus the people who were born here. Our neighborhood has lots of professionals. Tech people. They all throw up their hands and say, 'There's no one to vote for. The place is run by bumpkins.' There's no Four Seasons in the city of Napa, no Ritz Carlton, no Hyatt Regency just because *they don't want them here.* This is a resort community without resorts!"

"We couldn't even get a Trader Joe's," April said, referring to the discount gourmet supermarket chain that was a mainstay of northern California's BoBos.

The waiter brought a platter of risotto with seared scallops.

"Even Wal-Mart barely got through here," John said. "The whole place smells corrupt. I heard that the federal government was about to sue Napa County because it took forty million dollars for low-income housing that it never built. The migrant farmworkers don't have anyplace to live. Some of the workers live in their cars. There's not even *one* Habitat for Humanity project here, and they'll build it for you if you just give them some land! We really need a big celebrity to come in and point out the corruption and become the mayor, like Clint Eastwood did in Carmel or Sonny Bono in Palm Springs."

Then he began talking about "up valley."

"St. Helena doesn't want anyone who isn't *really* rich," he said.

"There are people with châteaux in the Napa hills who show up one or two times a season. It's like Newport, Rhode Island, during the heyday of the robber barons. There are only one or two big contractors, and they charge through the nose; they're impossible. The contractors are always working on mansions, but there's a sub-culture of good Mexican guys with no names on their trucks and they'll do your house for a good price in their spare time as a fill-in between the zillionaire jobs. We had them build a rock wall in our yard. They *sing* while they work."

THE LOCAL HERO for John Stallcup and his fellow Bobo invaders was the morning talk-show host on the AM radio station that broadcast from the city of Napa, KVON, which called itself "The Vine." The host's name was Jeff Schechtman. Almost daily he cru-saded against the backwardness and ignorance of the conservative Napkins who opposed investment and development of any kind. While Napa, like Sonoma, had its Babbitts encouraging outside de-velopers, in Napa it was the Napkins who played the role of the Yes Group, saying no to change. The difference, in my mind, was that the Napkins were plagued with a mindlessly ingrained conser-vatism, since their shabby city actually needed a lot of help, while the Yes Group justly wanted to preserve the character of their lovely town. The conservative Napkins and the liberal Yes activists wouldn't like each other, but they agitated for similar ends.

Jeff Schechtman had been a Hollywood player before he some-how wound up as the scathing Jewish troublemaker among the rambunctious rednecks. He was an executive at the New Line movie studio in Los Angeles. He was married to the producer Gale Anne Hurd, and after their divorce she remarried, to James Cameron, who had directed her famous *Terminator* movies.

The talk jock liked to have lunch at Celadon in downtown Napa. The bistro's East-West fusion cuisine and its airy design would have fit easily into any of San Francisco's upscale neighborhoods. It had an outdoor terrace that looked out at the greenery of the banks of the Napa River. The gentrifiers had pushed for millions of government dollars to prevent the river from flooding in the winter rainy seasons so that cafés like Celadon could thrive there.

Jeff Schechtman's confident stride and his slicked-back straight black hair recalled Michael Douglas as the rich corporate raider in the movie *Wall Street*. As Schechtman took his table, the chef-owner quickly emerged to greet him, as if crummy Napa were the kind of city where celebrities were treated like celebrities by chefs who themselves were celebrities. The place wasn't there yet, but that's where it was heading. The owner of Celadon had recently opened an upscale steakhouse next door, and a new Tuscan trattoria emerged across the street. Before long the inner core of the old downtown would become known as a foodie haven that diverted the New Yorkers and Angelenos who had always driven right by the city of Napa on their way to the wineries farther upvalley.

"Six years ago my girlfriend had had it with Los Angeles," Jeff said. "She had grown up in the Bay Area, and her mother was dying in San Francisco. So she moved back here. I came up on the weekends. We had a house in St. Helena at the time. I met Tom Young, who owned the radio station in the city of Napa. Tom asked me to do a weekend program on this little station. Then, three years ago, the morning slot opened up. I was fed up with Hollywood, so I said okay.

"The city of Napa was a very blue-collar, conservative place. It was the bedroom community for the Mare Island naval base. And as Napa has become a middle-class place, the old-timers haven't dealt with it well. There's real resentment, particularly now in downtown. There's a city council member, Henry Martin, with a constituency of old-timers, seniors. He has a newspaper that ferments class warfare against the elites. He can be very mean-spirited.

"You go to city council meetings and any time someone begins by saying 'I've been here thirty-five years,' nothing that comes after that is going to be good. These people always complain about the traffic, but there's *no* traffic. There are only three intersections where you ever have to wait.

"A year ago I left St. Helena and bought a house in the town of Napa itself. St. Helena and the upvalley are desperately trying to hang on to the past, like it's still the 1950s. St. Helena is a Stepford-like town. They like to think of themselves as a village with a 'small-town existence,' but they're in denial. They rely on tourists. They have Meadowood and Auberge du Soleil. They have an antitourist attitude, but that's like killing the goose with the golden eggs.

"St. Helena has rebuffed repeated attempts to make films there. St. Helena makes everything as difficult as possible. The city fathers and old-timers love to refer to St. Helena as a 'rural village.' But how many rural villages have an average house price of five hundred thousand dollars? When I lived up valley, I tortured the St. Helena City Council every week. We were happy to move from St. Helena to Napa, and it's thirty minutes closer to San Francisco.

"My personal sentiments lie with change and the business community. In downtown Napa we very much want it to become a 'latte town.' The growth advocates are winning. If the economy holds up, the revitalization will happen here and it will be very dramatic.

"But it's a problem that the low-income people are starting to get pushed out. The mobile-home parks in the Napa River's floodplain are being drained away. The Napa wine auction shows great generosity, and the vintners are happy to donate wine, but when it comes to giving money or doing something specific about the issue of farmworker housing, that's a different story."

AS IT BECAME notoriously hard to buy into the status of the Napa Valley, many of the plutocrats and the professionals began transferring their desires to nearby Sonoma, which seemed like a parallel universe. Sonoma had the same appealing microclimate—warm to hot in the daytime, pleasantly cool in the mornings and evenings, with hardly any humidity—and the same type of scenic beauty, with flat valley floors covered by vineyards and framed by mountain walls. Even Olle Lundberg, one of the most prominent architects building villas in Napa, said that the land in Sonoma was "even more spectacular."

Napa enjoyed greater international name recognition and cachet, but Sonoma had all the elements to become the new Napa. People who aspired to the Napa lifestyle but balked at Napa's prices and its barriers to entry—the impenetrable clubbiness, the tight lockdown on the land—were trying to re-create the dream in Sonoma much as the yuppies who found themselves shut out of the overpriced condos and snobby cooperative apartment buildings of Manhattan's Upper East Side in the eighties had gone west across Central Park and swiftly remade the Upper West Side in its image.

"There's frustration over finding parcels in Napa," Tim McDonald said. "There's a scarcity mentality. So a lot of people are going to Sonoma instead. We're going to do a house in Sonoma for the architect Robert A. M. Stern."

Sonoma had become the invasion's second front.

PART III

The Battle
for the Good Life

WHEN I FIRST ARRIVED as my wealthy friends' house guest in the spring of 2000, the Sonoma bohemians—galvanized by having saved their scenic hillside from exploitation—were launching four ambitious new political battles. The quartet of controversies turned the first year of the century into a crucial time of making choices about the future.

The first fight was for city hall. The activists already held two of the five positions on the city council. Two of their opponents from the Old Guard, who had served for many years and had tired of the constant burdens of the time-consuming unpaid positions, weren't running for reelection. If the Yes Group could capture even one of those two chairs, then they could take control of city government and use their newfound hegemony to repel the rich intruders.

Ditty Vella was the obvious choice for a candidate, since her impassioned political beliefs thrilled the other activists, and her old

Sonoma family name and her long personal history in the town endeared her to fellow natives.

But Ditty refused to run.

As her public explanation she said that she couldn't take on the responsibilities while raising and supporting her two sons, who were both still in high school. Privately, her friends suspected the real reason was that Ditty frequently became so infuriated by the ignorance and pigheadedness of political people and the maddeningly cumbersome process that she simply couldn't bear to serve in public office. She wouldn't even bring herself to attend city council meetings as an observer since the scene would surely infuriate her.

While Ditty withdrew herself from consideration, one of her compatriots announced his intentions. Joe Costello was Sonoma's version of the classic small-town lawyer. He was in his mid-fifties and had white hair, but remained youthfully slender, with a gentle, low-key, polite personality. He was as calm and measured and steady as Ditty and Tom Whitworth and Gary Edwards and Ken Brown were colorful and charismatic and incendiary. But his quiet determination was misleading, because Joe Costello was an extremist in his politics. He wanted a moratorium on all new development in the village of Sonoma.

Joe and his wife, Sandra, both grew up in the Midwest, and they spent their adult lives together trying to live in some kind of sunny paradise. After college they escaped to St. Thomas in the Virgin Islands, where Joe established his law practice. But when political upheavals and threats of violence forced them to carry revolvers when they went to the beach, the Costellos decided to seek nirvana in the safety of the mainland. They settled in Sonoma with its scenery and dry heat, living in an alley behind the historic Mission. When the Yes Group organized to save the hillside, which was only a few blocks from their small house, Joe joined early on. He was the one who actually drafted the Yes ballot referendum, and even though Tom and Gary were the provocateurs and the publicity mavens, Joe deserved a share of the credit.

The activists agreed that Joe was a good candidate and voiced their support. But they needed to find a second candidate to run along with him for the other chair.

The city of Sonoma was only a tiny part of the county of Sonoma, and who would sit on city council was only one of three important issues that the voters would decide in November. This time there were two new voter referendums, and like the Rosewood battle, they were about the dilemmas of preserving or developing open spaces.

Sonoma's environmentalists were proposing the Rural Heritage Initiative, which would ensure that eighty percent of the county's land remained rural for the next thirty years. Eighty percent was how much was currently zoned for agriculture. But the activists were worried that their elected politicians—the five members of the county's board of supervisors—could be swayed by the moneyed interests into making one exception after another for real-estate developers who wanted to build vast housing tracts and office parks in the place of old farmlands. The Rural Heritage Initiative was a radical effort by the citizens to strip away power from a government that they no longer trusted with their land.

If RHI passed, then anyone who wanted to change their zoning from rural to commercial or residential would have to seek approval from the voters in a countywide ballot. It wouldn't be enough anymore to make a big campaign contribution to a corruptible public official and then profit mightily from a return favor. The measure was similar to the Agriculture Preserve that protected the Napa Valley's lands, saving Napa from ruinous sprawl if not from a few architectural monstrosities.

RHI signaled a sense of urgency about safeguarding the future. Sonoma was still remarkably unspoiled, but the Yes activists knew how quickly things could change. Without the vigilant protection of its citizenry, Sonoma could be transformed completely within a generation, as the San Fernando and Santa Clara valleys had been.

The trend was beginning. Already the larger Petaluma River

Valley on the other side of Sonoma Mountain was becoming a boomtown known as "Telecom Valley" for its burgeoning cluster of international communications firms. The front page of the *Press-Democrat* ran the headline: "HIGH TECH PULLS EVEN WITH AG IN ECONOMIC CLOUT," reporting that "high tech rivals agriculture as the county's largest employer and most valuable industry." The county's 471 tech companies employed fifteen thousand workers and produced $1.1 billion of goods and services, while its agricultural businesses, including grape growing and winemaking, employed thirteen thousand people and produced $997 million. To the activists of Sonoma Valley, that proliferating Telecom Valley was a screaming wake-up call.

Even if the countywide Rural Heritage Initiative didn't pass, the Yes Group wanted to prevent the city council from letting their village encroach into the greenbelt of farms and vineyards and open spaces in their own valley. Tom Whitworth and Ditty Vella were among the leading supporters of the Urban Growth Boundary, or UGB, another acronym for the alphabet soup and another set of petitions that people were signing in order to put a referendum on the ballot in November. UGB would prevent the politicians from permitting the town to grow beyond its current constricting limits for the next twenty years. The village limits would be fixed firmly at about a mile and a half east-to-west as well as north-to-south.

The potential benefit from RHI and UGB was preserving the physical beauty of the place and the sense of community. But the risk was that by limiting growth, the measures would make the existing real estate in the towns more expensive, enriching the current property holders but making it prohibitive for any outsiders except the very rich to buy in. It meant protecting what the current residents adored about the place but closing the door to others who wanted it too. And it threatened the many people who rented but didn't own.

The fourth political battle of that season, and the most controversial and fundamentally divisive, had originated not in the Sonoma Valley in the southeast of the county but in another wine region, the Russian River Valley in the northwestern reaches, which was even more of a haven for environmental and peace activists, old hippies, New Agers, goddess worshippers, massage therapists, yogis, Buddhists, and other countercultural baby-boomer refugees from Haight-Ashbury and Berkeley. In the summers the slow, shallow river itself was filled with wading naked gay weekenders from San Francisco. It was like a summer camp for the Castro district, the city's celebrated epicenter of gay culture and politics.

The central town in the Russian River Valley was Sebastopol, and it was the only town in America where a majority of city council members openly belonged to Ralph Nader's leftist Green Party. Sebastopol's former mayor, Lynn Hamilton, had started a save-the-redwoods group when she was only eighteen. Now in her forties, she was leading a radical environmental activist group called the Town Hall Coalition. They had been holding meetings around the county to rally opposition not only against the real-estate developers but also, more surprisingly, against the wine grape growers.

Until recently the environmentalists had supported the wineries. The two camps had seemed like natural allies. As the county's traditional small dairies and produce farms were looking like endangered species, wine grapes became the only thing more profitable to grow there than houses. The Greens figured it was better for the land to be planted with leafy vines than paved over with split-levels and strip malls. But then they were shocked when Gallo, the nation's biggest and most powerful wine company, chopped down a stand of lovely old oak trees and razed a number of rolling hillsides to make way for vineyards. Although Gallo's behavior wasn't really typical of the larger community of Sonoma County vintners, its cavalier actions incited the activists to form a forceful movement. They demonized the grape growers for relying on pesticides that could be harmful to the vineyard workers and the residents. And now that a plague borne by an insect threatened to devastate the vines, some of the activists were rooting for nature to restore the land to its original state.

THE WEEK that I began staying at Celia's cottage on Fifth Street East, her neighbor Brad suggested that I drop by Sage Marketing to introduce myself to Ditty Vella, who was one of the town's ultimate insiders and perhaps the best person to give me an understanding of the political scene. Brad knew Ditty through two degrees of separation, which was the most it ever took in a town the size of Sonoma: Brad's wife Sue's brother Gary Edwards was Ditty's boyfriend and business colleague. I went there out of simple curiosity. I was eager enough to meet this Ditty if for no other reason than to see how a mature adult passed herself off as "Ditty." I had no premonition that the encounter would launch me into becoming an accidental activist in a place where I had just arrived.

I opened the front door and got sniffed by Ditty's large but benign dog, who served as a stand-in receptionist for the three-person firm. Ditty emerged from another room, and even before we sat down, I was fascinated by the way she looked. Ditty was fifty-one, and she was the mother of two teenage boys, but she seemed both much younger and much older than her actual age. She was so remarkably thin that she looked like a girl from junior high school who had just gone through a rapid growth spurt. And her toothy smile and her quick laughter were so joyous and buoyant that they made her seem like a free-spirited teenager or maybe a twentysomething hippie chick rather than a businessperson and mother with burdens and responsibilities. Her persona was utterly Californian, but her facial features were from the Old World. Her eyes were deeply set, her nose was long, and her cheeks were angular. It was a face you would expect to see if you were traveling in an ancient Sicilian fishing village or mountain hamlet where families had lived for countless centuries. It wasn't a face you'd expect of an assimilated American born after World War II. Only her hair—wedges that defied gravity as they shot in random directions—restored the impression that Ditty was a baby boomer.

Ditty led me into her office near the front of the cottage. She needed to be ready to take calls while we talked, so she sat behind her wooden desk, which had a lime-colored iMac computer with a yellow rubber toy duck on top. Ditty was a cheese broker, and every ten or fifteen minutes the phone would ring with a request from a supermarket chain for five hundred pounds of aged cow's-milk cheese or three hundred pounds of blue cheese and she would quote the current price and determine when they could deliver. She sold her family's cheeses and represented a bunch of other small producers, promoting them to the buyers at Whole Foods and other retailers across the country. She only worked with clients like Whole Foods who would let her wear jeans to business meetings. She refused to wear corporate drag. If a business suit was expected, she left the account to Gary.

I had met plenty of stockbrokers and commodity brokers before, but I had never heard of a cheese broker.

She gestured for me to sit in a wood chair in the corner. I cleared the seat, removing a pamphlet for the International Slow Food Movement, a phenomenon that began in Italy a few years earlier. Ditty belonged to the Sonoma "cell" of the movement, which called for a cultural and gastronomic revolution, a return to a lost way of life that centered on fine natural foods from local producers rather than banal processed foods and fast foods from agribusiness monoliths.

Before sitting down, I noticed a green bumper sticker pasted to seat of the chair: "RHI: The Sprawl Stops Here," it said.

"My main point for you," Ditty began, "is that people are coming in and spending a lot of money for houses that those of us who grew up here can't afford. And then these people come here only on the weekends. It's a real detriment to the community."

Ditty talked quickly, with an animated energy that conveyed her passion for her causes.

"It's appalling when so many houses are empty during the week, and the owners aren't involved at all in the town," she said. "Giving back to the community is such an important part of living in a small town. We're the people who make it real here. If we can't afford to live here, it becomes just another resort. I've rented a house on the east side for eleven years, but now I can't afford it. I'm going to have to move out of the house where I raised my kids."

She was interrupted by a call. It was an activist telling her that a developer was trying to put up five hundred houses on a cow pasture near the border between Sonoma and Marin counties. Ditty was agitated and angry as she hung up.

"These city people come with tons of money and build these big houses and paint them awful colors because they think that makes it look like Tuscany."

"What do you think about those big houses at Armstrong Estates?" I asked.

"We don't know anyone who lives there," she said. "I'm not of that strata. I don't know anyone who would spend their money that way."

Ditty explained that as part of the town's deal to allow Steve Ledson to build Armstrong Estates, he had to put a small public park on the site. It was supposed to serve the entire populace, not just the wealthy residents of his enormous houses. Ledson built the park, but for a long time he kept it blocked by construction fencing, preventing the poorer people from across town from taking their children to the little playground. "We wanted to hold a Cinqo de Mayo party there with lots of Latinos and boom boxes," Ditty said, and the mischievous idea seemed to banish her anger and restored her sense of joyfulness. Because Ledson was a Sonoma native

as well as the impresario of the new-money crowd, he was the in-
timate enemy of Ditty's friends, their Darth Vader.

"There was an empty field right next to the Armstrong Estates,
and the owners proposed twenty houses that would sell in the high
six figures. Well, the Armstrong people were livid because they had
paid *millions* for their houses, and they didn't want the 'riff-raff'
driving through their neighborhood."

I asked Ditty about the Town Hall Coalition.

"A couple of the members of our Yes Group are antivineyard,"
Ditty said. "We call them 'environmental Nazis,'" she continued,
laughing out loud. "But my view is that without the vineyards, the
pressure for more housing would be much worse. It doesn't matter
what the zoning calls for. If the financial return isn't there for small
farms, there won't be small farms. Agriculture on a small scale is
backbreaking work. And in today's world, in our northern California economy, I don't see many people willing to work that way.

"The vintners are being slammed now. They're criticized for using pesticides. I feel for them, because they've always been a low-
key and generous part of the community. They give to lots of
causes. Any charity event that asks, they give. Sonoma's wealth is
older and quieter than Napa's. The Sebastianis are very quiet about
supporting the town. It's always no strings, and they never want
their name attached. The vintners have an old-fashioned philan-
thropic vein. But still, there's a certain validity to the arguments
against them. So they have to change their tactics. They have to become more vocal about their contributions."

Ditty faced toward her window. Her little office used to be
flooded with sunshine, but now it looked out on a banal seven-
foot-high concrete wall hardly a foot away that blocked the direct
light. The eyesore had been erected by the builders of the three-
story upscale shopping complex rising next door, which was
painted in the clichéd Tuscan orange hue. Ditty and Gary had opposed the charmless hulking structure because it would overwhelm

the modest scale of their own building, a cottage that had served as the town's first library a century ago and still helped sustain the quaint character of the blocks surrounding the Plaza. So the developers put up an especially ugly wall as an act of vengeful retribution. When Gary was in a bad mood, he called it "the Berlin Wall."

Near Ditty's desk I noticed a photo of her and Gary skiing in the Alps. "People ask me how can I afford to go on a three-week vacation to Europe every year with my kids," Ditty said. "Well, I paint my own house, and I wear old clothes. I cook my own food, and I buy few prepared foods, and I don't eat out. I don't have TV. I would rather read instead."

Already I decided that I liked Ditty for her passionate temperament as well as her realism and pragmatism. But I was still concerned that she would be suspicious of me because I was a friend of those city people with tons of money who bought houses and came only on weekends. So I was surprised and pleased when Ditty invited me to take part in the next Yes political meeting. I had never belonged to a group of agitators and activists, but then again, never before had I found one whose members shared my fervor for fine cheeses.

ABOUT TWO DOZEN PEOPLE, apparently unburdened by the outmoded need to be at work during the daytime, were gathered at ten o'clock on a weekday morning at the outdoor amphitheater at the Plaza, discussing ideas for the hillside trail they were going to build on the site where the out-of-town developers wanted to put a luxury resort. Everyone agreed that the trail had to be "minimally intrusive" to the environment.

I said hello to Ditty, who was wearing blue jeans and a T-shirt without brand logos. She looked at me suspiciously, and I was taken aback at first. Then I realized that she was scrutinizing my outfit. I was a walking advertisement today.

"Sonoma Spa," she said. "The Girl and the Fig."

I was wearing a T-shirt with the large logo of the spa on the Plaza where I had started going for expensive massage treatments. And my cream-colored cotton baseball hat was inscribed with the name of the pricey local restaurant where I had my lavish dinner last night: a salad of dried figs, arugala, pecans, and Sonoma goat cheese followed by a braised leg and thigh and pan-roasted loin of Sonoma rabbit with artichoke pan sauce, basil-scented potato cakes, and baby carrots, and finally a lavender-flavored crème brûlée.

Unwittingly I had flaunted my spending in front of a group of local activists who opposed the town's elitist invasion. I had revealed myself as an emissary of the enemy.

Ditty must have wondered whether I was more like her or more like Celia. It wasn't that the Yes people were against the hedonistic pursuits. Ditty got a massage every week or two, but it was from someone who served only the locals, not from a costly joint that targeted the rich tourists. Ditty and her teenage sons ate as well on a daily basis as anyone I knew, but that was because she shopped at the farmer's market and cooked from scratch instead of going out on a regular basis to expensive restaurants.

One of the great virtues of Sonoma was that it offered the good life on the cheap. For the members of the Yes Group, who were writers and artists and craftspeople and environmentalists and organic farmers and other assorted varieties of iconoclasts, Sonoma was one of the rare remaining bohemias, and I began feeling a bit guilty about my association with the potentates who were pushing out the poets.

On the agenda that morning was a tiumphant celebratory hike up the hillside they had preserved. The Yes Group was exploring and enjoying the very site that they saved from development and exploitation.

The trail's architect led us through the dense woods. His name was Jim Jacobson, and at that point the trail existed exclusively in his imagination, his topographical drawings, and in the sight lines only he could discern between the red flags that he had planted into the earth at wide intervals and that were obscured by the brush and the trees. Jim was slim and bearded and tranquil to the point of detachment. He looked as though he could survive in the woods effortlessly for months without the aid of provisions or the stimulation of human contact.

In contrast, I was uncomfortable because I couldn't stop thinking about the inevitability of spending the next month scratching the poison oak rashes that would surely cover much of my body. Poison oak seemed to be everywhere. Eventually, when the Yes Group built the trail, they would have to remove a lot of rocks to make a smooth, walkable surface, but mostly they would have to cut away and remove a few tons of poison oak.

"We'll need to pull out the roots within ten feet of the trail," Jim said.

About a dozen activists were following him through the woods and brush. He led us behind the town's nineteenth-century cemetery and past a ravine that the rednecks had turned into a de facto dump several decades ago. In the intervening years most of the discarded junk has been covered with vegetation, but Jim wanted to bring in a pickup truck to take out the larger pieces of debris, like the abandoned metal top of an old car that stood like a piece of sculpture.

I walked alongside Will Shonbrun, who lived in the bohemian precincts of the Springs and edited a scrappy newsletter called the *Sonoma Valley Voice*, a liberal alternative to the establishment's *Index-Tribune* newspaper.

We saw Tom Whitworth emerging through the woods. He arrived at the trailhead too late for the rendezvous, so he had to find his own way through the trees.

"Where were you?" Will asked him.

"Founding a new country where there's a chicken in every Plaza," Tom deadpanned.

Will grinned. "It's called Cannard Land."

Tom launched into a monologue as we continued to walk. He

was exuberant and animated and he seemed to relish the roles of jokester and commentator. He told an anecdote about the vineyard workers, who lately had been wearing special clothing and gear to shield their eyes and skin while they sprayed the vines with sulfur, which prevented a mildewy fungus from infecting the leaves, shoots, and flowers of the unripe grapes. Their bulky white suits and plastic helmets made them look like astronauts walking on the surface of the moon.

"Some of the locals were scared when they saw the suits," Tom said. "I had to tell them those aren't *aliens*, they're just *resident aliens*."

The others gave him a Tom-will-be-Tom kind of smile.

We ascended through the woods and arrived at the first large clearing, a steep meadow covered with bright yellow Mariposa lilies. Looking down we could see the leafy clusters of the town surrounded by the open farmlands of the valley. It was the kind of panoramic view you would expect from an $800-a-night luxury hotel suite, but now it was being donated to future hikers for free.

The sight was having a powerful effect on us. Suddenly Tom stopped his irreverent joking and began to prophesize out loud about environment and economic development and politics and the future. He swept his arm in a grand gesture.

"In forty years this will all be covered by houses," he said. "The world is too close. You look at Beverly Hills and other places in California where the canyons are heavily populated, and you can see that happening here. It's inevitable because development is rushing forward. Every year we say it's a turning point. You realize that you have to push hard. The county's supervisors are not used to saying no to developers. We're trying to hold it back with RHI and UGB. We can't stop it, but we *can* hold it back for most of our lifetime."

From our elevated vantage point the town's houses and streets seemed well shaded by its trees in most places, but the glaring exception was the clearance for the Armstrong Estates, the houses in which stood out conspicuously for their arrogant sizes.

"House sizes are increasing while family sizes are decreasing," Tom said.

"I still live in the same nine-hundred-square-foot house where I raised my two kids," Ditty said. "I wouldn't want more interior space. I'd rather have a garden."

Ditty looked down at people walking and bicycling on the path where the train tracks used to be back when she was growing up, and she turned nostalgic.

"When we were kids we'd put pennies on the track and run away."

We descended through the oldest part of the cemetery, slowing down to read the names on the tombstones of people born in the mid-nineteenth century. The Sebastiani dynasty had two large monuments. I saw the family tomb of the Remezzanos, with several generations of the ancestors of the olive-oil couple from the farmer's market, Mike and Allison O'Donnell. Even though they now have an Irish surname, they used Remezzano as their olive-oil brand name. The Italians in town often intermarried with the Irish, who were fellow Catholics, rather than with the Protestant Germans, who were members of the merchant class. The Vallejos, the Mexican family that once owned all of the Sonoma Valley, also intermarried with the Irish and sustained a long Spanish-Irish line. General Mariano Vallejo's only surviving direct descendent was named Martha McGettigan.

We came to Vallejo's stately tomb.

"We saved your hillside, Mariano," Will said. "I hope you're happy!"

When we emerged from the cemetery, some people dispersed to their bikes and cars, but a few of us walked together to Wild Thyme, a café near the Plaza. As soon as Ditty entered, she began scrutinizing the cheeses in the refrigerator displays. Tom and Will took a table and talked happily, seemingly unconcerned about the poison oak we had spent an hour traipsing through, but I was still nervous about it. I rushed to the men's room, wet down a pile of paper towels, and scrubbed my exposed arms, hands, neck, and face with a manic desperation.

THE INNER CIRCLE of the Yes Group called for a small meeting to talk with a man named Dick Ashford, who was running for a seat on the city council and sought the group's endorsement. Ditty's boyfriend, Gary Edwards, was hosting the get-together, and around five o'clock I parked in front of his single-story house on the east side. Gary was in his forties and he was seen as the young fellow on the block. He lived across from a woman who was 104 and had lived there for sixty years.

Gary was standing in his yard, watering his flowers with a garden hose. Dick walked up, looking healthy and fit for his sixties. He was well-groomed with his short-clipped hair and very crisply turned out in a polo and pressed khaki pants. As a continuous forceful stream of water poured forth from the hose, Gary appeared embarrassed that he was wasting water in front of a political candidate whose big issue was water conservation in an arid valley struggling with too much growth.

"You ought to put that on a drip," Dick advised with a gentle tone.

We entered the house and sat at Gary's dining table, looking out the window at the backyard with its huge Monterey pines and its lovely roses and its two ninety-year-old pear trees. Ditty and Tom and a couple of others joined us at the table. We were all wearing completely different clothing than we wore in the poison oak on the hillside earlier in the day.

The meeting began, and Dick described his background. He was a naval officer for twenty-three years and then spent a decade teaching naval officers at a special school at the nearby shipyard and base, which recently closed down. Now, in his retirement, he was a passionate bird-watcher and he volunteered as a docent at the wetlands nature center run by a branch of the Sebastiani wine family.

"I'm concerned about companies like Cisco and Nokia creating jobs in Telecom Valley that will lead to increased water demand," he said. "And the new Marriott hotel is drilling deep down, seven hundred feet, for a well that will pump fifteen thousand gallons a day because they don't want to rely on the city's water."

"There's nothing you can do about it," Tom said, "because anyone can dig a well."

"But they're getting city development money," Gary shot back. When Sonoma blocked the Rosewood developers from putting a hotel on the hillside, the town tried to counteract the blow and appease the business community by allowing Marriott to go ahead with a large hotel on the flats near the outskirts of town. The thinking was that this new complex could accommodate the kind of "off-site" retreats favored by the many free-spending companies from Silicon Valley. But now the project threatened to soak up too much of the underground water tables. The city had other sources of water, but the people who lived in the nearby rural areas had to rely on their own wells, which tapped into the aquifer.

"The trouble," Tom said, "is that for people who live outside the city limits, like me, the water won't be there anymore."

Gary lifted one of several bottles of imported sparkling mineral water.

"That's why I'm serving Italian water today," he joked. "We're redistributing the world's supply of water!"

"When I was on the environmental board, we mandated xeriscape," Ditty said, referring to a style of landscaping that didn't require any watering. "And then Ledson built his Pleasantville"—the Armstrong Estates—"and he planted magnolias as street trees! The problem is that most people perceive xeriscape as cacti."

"Worse, as red volcanic rocks!" Gary interjected, and everyone joined in laughter at the image of bad taste he had conveyed in a single short phrase.

"Can we have those red rocks banned in Sonoma?" Gary joked.

"The University of California at Davis has a xeriscape garden that you can see as a demonstration," Dick said, "and it's pretty."

"More and more of the town is going to be paved," Ditty said. "And as there are more buildings and more concrete, we'll need French wells if we're going to preserve the aquifer."

"Everyone's got to have a tank in their yard," Gary said, "or a barrel."

The group asked the candidate about his position on the Urban Growth Boundary.

"So far I'm neutral on it," Dick said. "I won't take a position yet."

"Our group met with the UGB people," Gary said, "and we're not going to take a position as a group."

The UGB voter referendum had divided the activists. A few of them opposed it because they believed that sharply limiting the city's growth would make the existing real estate much more expensive and force out everyone except the rich.

"Personally, I support the Urban Growth Boundary," Tom said. "But I can see the problems it might bring. It could lead to a zooming up of land prices. But I'll be *damned* if I want to leave matters in the hands of the elected officials!"

The meeting ended, and Gary took me on a walk around the corner to call on Ig Vella. We found the cheesemaker sitting at his kitchen table while his wife, Sally, boiled water for pasta and prepared a salad of greens and carrots. And like everyone else in Sonoma, they were gossiping about house prices.

"That two-story house next to Brad and Sue Gross sold for eight hundred fifty thousand in one week!" she said.

I glanced around Ig and Sally's home, which was remarkably modest in its scale and decor. It seemed more like the house of a grandfather living off Social Security than a leader of local commerce. They owned a prosperous business in town, a large ranch in the rural reaches of the valley, and a factory in another state, and yet their own living space was smaller than my friend Ann Winblad's pool house, and they were upset that other people with their kind of money would actually spend it.

ON THE TRAIL HIKE I quickly realized that Tom Whitworth had the same qualities that I liked so much about Ditty Vella: He was similarly exuberant and effusive, irreverent and intelligent, with an enlightened realism about the encroaching world that nonetheless didn't inhibit him from striving with passionate idealism to try to preserve Sonoma's anachronistic character. I offered to buy Tom lunch the following week anywhere he'd like around the town, thinking that he'd take advantage of my largesse by picking an upscale spot near the Plaza, like Meritage. Instead he invited me to a dive on the outskirts.

The Ranch House was a roadside shack, albeit a shack with a clear view of Sonoma Mountain from across an expanse of vineyards. It was the familiar kind of Mexican diner that got its tortillas from a bag and salsas from a bottle rather than making everything fresh, but the place had a homey friendliness.

"I used to be an advertising guy in a suit," Tom began, and as I looked at him, with his subversive glint and his old T-shirt, it was hard to imagine him putting up with the conformity of corporate life, even in a field known for creativity.

"I worked in advertising and marketing for General Foods and other multinational corporations in London," he continued. "I was also an amateur actor. I was part of a troupe that put on plays in little villages on Oxfordshire. The government gave us grants to bring live theater to these small towns.

"When I was in my mid-thirties, I played opposite a twenty-one-year-old Argentine girl, Maria. She was extraordinarily attractive. Her mother had moved from Buenos Aires to Berkeley, and Maria said, 'Let's do it in Berkeley.' It was my first time in the U.S. I thought Berkeley was great. I loved San Francisco. I got a job there at Ogilvy Advertising. I had a nice apartment in Pacific Heights and a wife who was fourteen years younger than I was, and I was partying for years.

"But after a while the marriage faded. Maria moved to New York. And I wasn't satisfied with my career. I wanted to switch from account management to the creative side, so I went out on my own—just as the market took a downturn.

"And then I almost died in a motorcycle accident.

"I had rebuilt a British Triumph 650 Trophy and I liked hanging out with motorcycle people. I had just finished doing ten storyboards for Sprint ads for J. Walter Thompson. I delivered them and then went to South Park for a cigarette with my crazy friend Eddie who owned a building there. And then, two minutes later, I was in a wreck. It was a massive hit-and-run accident at Fifth and Harrison.

"Everything was broken, and my internal injuries were awful. I could hardly speak because my lungs had collapsed. They told my eighteen-year-old son, Miles, not to expect me to live.

"I was lying there and I knew I was close to death. I thought: I've had an incredibly fantastic life. I've had a great time, and it doesn't matter if it stops.

"But then I decided to make the effort to live.

"It took three years to recover. I was in a wheelchair, and I needed to be somewhere flat. Maria's mother, my ex-mother-in-law, was in Sonoma, and the town was very flat. After a year here, I decided to stay. I never went back to live in the city again. Coming close to dying made me more concerned about natural pleasures like walking by the greenery of the vineyards. The accident and living here made me want to have much more contact with the natural world.

"I rekindled my love of the outdoors. I learned to draw, and now I make a living as a designer. After the accident I *couldn't* work hard but I found that I could get by in Sonoma. I did T-shirt designs about the environment, and that led to illustrations for museum projects. I gained confidence in my artistic abilities. I worked on a natural history museum in Seattle. I did projects for Yosemite."

I asked how he met his girlfriend, Jeri Lynn Chandler, who worked as an assistant at the *Index-Tribune*. She had stopped by the other day when we were at Wild Thyme, which was next door to the newspaper's offices. Jeri was forty but she looked more like thirty. She was fair-skinned, tall, slender, long-legged, an understated natural beauty with perfectly proportioned features and long straight brown hair.

"I loved to sit at the Plaza for hours with my coffee and my dogs, and that's where I met Jeri three years ago," Tom told me. "She had gone to Berkeley to get a master's in landscape architecture, but she got disillusioned with the institution. She came to Sonoma to garden and landscape with her boyfriend.

"A few weeks after I met her, I said, 'I know you're in a relationship, but if you want to get away, I have an extra room upstairs.'

"One day she turned up with her cat and all of her belongings in a truck.

"Sonoma is said to be the place for people without a plan. 'Slow-noma.' You get sucked in by the sun and the hanging out at the Plaza, and you find a way to live cheaply.

"This place will become another expensive resort like Carmel. It will, in the long run, but in the meantime we can squeeze out our pleasure here. The Rosewoods of the world will try to get in here, so we have to combat them more strongly. The Yes on Measure A vote was a turning point and now people see that they can be more aggressive. I don't know what it's going to take to pass the Rural Heritage Initiative and the Urban Growth Boundary, but we're starting the battles. It's the age-old struggle of the people versus the special interests.

"People raise the issue of 'NIMBYism' about development, 'not in my backyard,' but I don't think there's anything wrong with being selfish about where you live. In Sonoma, for the first time anywhere, I've been able to say 'five years ago' and feel a sense of place.

If we can preserve the little things here, we can hang on for another twenty years. I don't think you can maintain this area the way the old people remember, but you *can* have some foresight.

"The world is like a Ouija board with everyone having a finger on the glass: No one person can control things, but there are trends. America is going toward gloss and entertainment, but on a local level there are fewer fingers on the Ouija board, and you *can* have influence. Some people disagree with the Urban Growth Boundary and say that if their kids want to change things in twenty years, they should be able to. But in America democracy has to try to regulate the excesses of capitalism. All I ask of local government is to keep the excesses of capitalism from rearing their ugly heads in our own little world.

"When we put Measure A on the ballot, I was really turned on by the movement. For me, to be honest, it was a way to put together a lot of skills I had acquired over the years, and I fed off the energy of the people. We were all terrified that we would lose, so we really put the pressure on.

"I think that rural charm is the heart of Sonoma, and it's really important to hang on to some of the eccentricity. The chickens in the Plaza are a way of preserving our silliness and keeping people involved in the center of the town. I take a perverse delight in fighting with city hall, and I am determined to devote my entire summer, if necessary, to crusading for the return of the chickens."

We finished our overstuffed burritos, said goodbye, and drove off separately. Later in the day Tom and Jeri Lynn spotted me at the farmer's market and came by to schmooze. Ditty Vella soon joined us, and then Ken Brown completed the circle.

"You should have heard my speech yesterday at the Memorial Day service," Ken said proudly. He was wearing sandals and shorts and a black T-shirt.

"I gave the vets what they like to hear: blood, guts, and glory," Ken went on, swinging his fist through the air with a swooping undercut. The gesture was unintentionally funny because it was nearly impossible to envision Ken in the macho ranks of the armed forces, wielding a gun or shouting profanities or driving a tank. The man didn't even own a car. He had lived for a quarter-century within a block of the Plaza, and he got around town on foot or on bicycle.

"We had three hundred veterans looking up at the hillside from the cemetery. It was really moving," he said seriously. Then there was a brief pause and he smiled subversively and said in a comical tone: "Can you imagine if they were looking at rich resort people?"

We all laughed together, and I realized that I was grinning with them, even though I was about to return to housesitting at the estate of my centimillionaire venture-capitalist friend with her private robot-cleaned lap pool and her hot tub and her own shady tennis court with an automatic ball machine.

I had been in this place for only a month, but already I felt a strong identification with these people and their idealistic struggles. I wanted them to bring the chickens back to the Plaza. I wanted them to safeguard this quirky little village from turning into yet another casualty of suburban sprawl. I wanted this valley and the half-dozen other valleys in the county to be preserved in their natural beauty rather than becoming the next frontiers of urbanization. I wanted these activists to win their voter initiatives in November. I wanted their candidates to take over the city council and to preserve this town the way it was now. I had met the enemy, and now, I was taking sides.

THROUGH THAT SUMMER and autumn I became one of the regulars at Tom and Jeri Lynn's Thursday dinners. Tom usually cooked spaghetti. Ditty and Gary came sometimes, and so did Ditty's fifteen-year-old son, Marius, who made and flew kites and model planes with Tom, who was something of a fifteen-year-old himself. Their neighbor Pete was a frequent guest and I talked with him about how mind-altering drugs had inspired the fantastically colorful and creative folk art of the Mexican province of Oaxaca and how a respected Berkeley professor, Houston Smith, who was a leading scholar of world religions and a bestselling author, defended psychedelics as a legitimate way of achieving profound spiritual experiences. Pete and Tom would smoke some marijuana after dinner while Jeri and I drank red wine. They'd serve an exceptionally fresh blackberry-peach pie that Jeri had made from blackberries Tom picked by reaching over a neighbor's fence, and Pete would talk about how he could lie back in his yard, open his mouth, and bite at the fresh figs that fell down from the trees, as though he were in a latter-day Eden.

Pete entertained us with descriptions of limousines pulling up to Harry's house and hairy men coming out wearing high heels and diapers and carrying baby bottles. When Harry wasn't engaging in infantile regression, he was a manly figure. His garage was equipped like a complete auto-body shop, and Pete went over often to borrow from his astonishing array of tools. And Harry generously allowed poor hippie types to camp out for free on his property.

Tom was always eager to show off some new sketch or design he had created. He was working on political advertisements for Dick Ashford's city council race and for the Urban Growth Boundary and the Rural Heritage Initiative. He was a one-man propaganda machine for Sonoma's activists, taking the skills of manipulation and influence that he had developed in the corporate world and applying them to his new subversive causes.

But Tom felt resentment against the Yes Group's own candidate, Joe Costello, in a surprising turn that marked the first rift in the solidarity of the movement. The split was precipitated after a Tuesday night farmer's market in July, when Joe gave Tom a copy of the supposed "book" he had written—it was really more of a long essay—about the history of the Measure A battle. Tom was incensed because Joe portrayed himself as the great hero and hardly mentioned Tom.

And earlier that night Joe had taken something of a grandstanding turn at the farmer's market in a special sideshow of an event called Short-Order Poetry. As a charity event for the Sonoma Valley Poetry Festival, some local writers gathered on the lawn in front of city hall and volunteered to compose verses on the spot. The patrons made $5 to $15 donations and came up with the "ingredients"—three words or phrases—and the writers turned them into short-order poems and read their work over a loudspeaker to the farmer's market crowd, which included just about everyone you knew. And so, as a generous public stunt to show his political support, Ken Brown ordered a poem in honor of Joe with the key words "Joe Costello and Yes for Sonoma City Council." A few minutes later, a poet read this over the microphone:

> There was a citizen named Costello
> Who yearned for a town most mellow
> So when outsiders arrived
> to build a hotel on the side
> of our hill, he roused with a bellow
> it was Measure A, and turned their plans to Jell-O.

Joe was the front man, and he was getting the credit—and taking it—but Tom and Gary had always seen themselves as the hidden persuaders and manipulators. Joe's calm personality and his conservative outward demeanor made him a better figurehead than Tom with his mischievous eyes and excitable temper and his penchant for public stunts and troublemaking. But Tom was becoming resentful that Joe had such a spotlight.

After that Tuesday night the two men weren't speaking.

THE YES GROUP lost more of its solidarity as the summer progressed. Tom Whitworth managed to reconcile with Joe Costello but their falling out revealed for the first time that the movement, which had seemed so inspired and idealistic, was nonetheless as human and political as any other, as vulnerable to personality conflicts and wounded egos, credit grabbing and petty rivalries.

Then there was the problem of finding a candidate to support for the second open seat on the city council. At first the Yes activists were excited by Dick Ashford, who had unimpeachable qualifications as an environmentalist, but over time some of them became suspicious, especially since Dick refused to announce a public position on the Urban Growth Boundary, which suggested that he might secretly oppose it. The Yes people worried that Dick seemed too cozy with the business interests. It seemed that he might be trying to play to both sides, which made him at worst deceitful or at best a shrewdly conciliatory moderate who could be a unifier of disparate camps. Neither scenario appealed to the ideologues. And a few of the more paranoid activists started speculating that Dick had served as an intelligence agent, a spy for the U.S. government. They wondered aloud whether his long résumé of responsible positions in the military could have been a cover for his real work with the Central Intelligence Agency. There was no evidence that Dick was a retired spook, but it was such an intriguing idea that people gossiped about it.

If they didn't trust Dick Ashford, then the Yes Group had to rely solely on Joe Costello's candidacy, which was somewhat worrisome. While Joe was sweet-tempered and thoroughly likeable, he was rather lacking in charisma. And the stakes seemed even higher when the business establishment revealed that it would be represented by a formidable candidate: Jim Ghilotti.

Ghilotti ran a large firm that was one of the most powerful and highly visible construction contractors in the entire region from Sonoma down to San Francisco. He had very publicly lobbied for the plans for a Rosewood hotel on the hillside—not surprisingly, since his company was the likeliest choice to build the resort. (Of course, Ghilotti's new campaign literature for his city council bid made no mention of his Rosewood failure. He co-opted the themes of his opponents by claiming that he would work hard to "protect our hillsides and small-town charm.")

He was smart and combative, and his persona—pillar of the community, four-square family man, and no-bullshit regular guy—made him especially appealing to the natives and the small-town Babbittry. He was an icon of evil to the bohemians, partly because of the Rosewood episode, but more recently because his firm was the contractor for the major expansion of Sears Point Raceway, a NASCAR venue on one of the main routes into the valley. It was, inescapably, one of the gateways to Sonoma. For years the bohemians had hated the white-trashy image of Sears Point and how rudely it marred the scenic beauty of the wetlands and vineyards nearby. But in its original form the complex was mostly hidden behind a series of rolling hills. Now it was building out so it would be much more visible from the roadway and more intrusive into the natural environment, and the Yes people were incensed. Every time they drove by, they saw massive Dumpsters and large pieces of construction equipment painted in eye-catching bright colors and emblazoned with the Ghilotti name. He had become their worst enemy, and he had a good chance of preventing them from getting a majority on the council.

Ghilotti was everything that the bohemians were not, the meat-and-potatoes to their goat cheese and radicchio. He was beefy while they were skinny; he was clean-shaven while their men were fully bearded or perennially scruffy. He campaigned on an image of tradition, respectability, and family values. "Jim's top priority, and his greatest strength, is his family," said the slick campaign brochure that he mailed to everyone in town. He had two toothy, wholesome teenage children—a blonde daughter who was a junior in high school and a buzz-cutted son at St. Mary's, a nearby Catholic college—and he was about to celebrate his twenty-fifth wedding anniversary with his first and only wife, who looked like a throwback to the 1950s. In contrast, the local gossips knew that Ken

Brown was already on his fourth wife, Gary Edwards was twice divorced, and both men had even moved coast-to-coast to escape from failing relationships. Ditty Vella was divorced from a man who was undeniably a little strange, and Tom Whitworth was divorced and currently living with a younger woman who had left her longtime boyfriend for him.

Ghilotti was a regular at the St. Francis Catholic Church, where he played leadership roles on the parish council and the parochial school board. He even included a photograph of the chapel in his campaign ads. The bohemians weren't churchgoers, and Ken's wife was so "crunchy" that she could have been some kind of pagan for all anyone knew.

Ghilotti was the third generation of an immigrant Sonoma family and he was carrying on the tradition of the business founded by his grandfather in the 1910s. The bohemians were mostly transplants who had abandoned their original careers.

Ghilotti extolled a sense of duty and social debt: The headline on the cover of his flyer proclaimed "It's About Giving Back." The bohemians seemed like chronic narcissists. They were lifelong seekers of hedonistic self-fulfillment.

Ghilotti stressed the competence, seriousness, and experience of an engineer who, along with his brother, ran a firm with 325 employees and $50 million in annual revenues. "As a businessman, I know how to manage complex budgets and I will use my expertise to make sure every tax dollar is spent efficiently," he said in a campaign statement. The bohemians were led by renegade marketing and P.R. hypsters who loved rambunctious pranks and grandstanding stunts.

Ghilotti's color scheme for his campaign signs and flyers was a patriotic red, white, and blue; the Yes Group adopted the dark green of the environmentalists on the left.

Ghilotti's favorite pastime was hunting. The bohemians preferred hiking in the woods, without having to kill anything. Ghilotti rode a noisy Harley-Davidson motorcycle. For charity events at Sears Point he relished drag racing in a pickup truck painted with red flames. Ditty Vella, Ken Brown, and Mayor Larry Barnett preferred steering their nearly noiseless bicycles around the Plaza; Ken didn't even own a car.

Jim Ghilotti's candidacy was what Tom Whitworth and Gary Edwards needed to reinvigorate their own efforts. They needed to put a face on the opposition. They needed a formidable opponent to provide a sense of challenge and urgency. And they needed someone to demonize. Just as they had enjoyed despising their neighboring store owner Alexis Gray during the Rosewood fight, they loved the idea of beating Ghilotti.

Tom began talking about the campaign posters they might put up later in the fall as the election approached. Ghilotti's name was pronounced exactly like the Italian word "gelati," the plural of "gelato," a dessert that resembled American ice cream but was even richer and creamier. So, next to the "Ghilotti for City Council" posters Tom would post "Ghilotti for Ice Cream!" No one was quite sure whether Tom was joking or whether his scheme was actually a strategy for attracting the attention of foodies who voted. If that's the best he can do, I thought, then the bohemians are in trouble.

THE CAMPAIGNS LAUNCHED formally in late August with the candidates' fund-raising events, which reflected their personalities and politics with nearly cinematic perfection.

Joe Costello held his official debut aboard a four-hour riverboat cruise on a Sunday afternoon. The awkwardly hulking craft was an ersatz version of the old Mississippi steam-powered paddleboats with their narrow black smokestacks and triple-tiered decks and ornate railings. The boat, a tourist gimmick, was called the *California Wine Ship*. It docked in the Carneros wetlands on a slough that snaked through muddy shallow waterbeds to San Pablo Bay, the northernmost extension of the more famous geography of San Francisco Bay.

"The boat was donated by one of Joe's former law clients who owed him money," Ditty Vella told me bemusedly as we waited to board. "The client donated the boat and the crew, the beer and the wine, and maybe even the band," she said. "Gary brought extra wine and cheeses just in case."

As we walked the gangway and entered the main ballroom on the lower deck, the bohemians were overwhelmed by the conspicuous bad taste of it all. There were mirrored walls around the dance floor and a reflective 1970s disco ball on the ceiling. The band, led by an accordion player, was awful. It wasn't high camp. It wasn't a bunch of sophisticates exulting in kitsch culture. It was just unintentionally bad.

"This is *so* tacky," Gary Edwards exclaimed. He was carrying a platter of expensive cheeses and he looked embarrassed about bringing such fine food into this place.

"What is this, a bar mitzvah?" moaned Ken Brown.

The crowd included Ken's wife, Jewel, Tom and Jeri Lynn, and Dick Ashford, and Mary Sullivan, the winemaker from Sebastiani. We tried to talk on the open-air top deck but the preprogrammed tinny organ pipes kept playing the same loud and cloying melodies. And there was no escape: It was a four-hour cruise. The boat was so slow that it couldn't get anywhere near the great sights like the Bay Bridge and the Golden Gate Bridge and Alcatraz. It only made it as far as a stretch of old garbage dumps and petroleum refineries. Some of the bohemians considered jumping overboard and attempting to swim back home. But their fellow-travelers from the town—well-off retirees with environmental concerns—seemed to be enjoying the long ride. They smiled as though this were the best possible way to spend a Sunday afternoon. There were 179 paying attendees who bought tickets for $10 each, so Joe Costello raised $1,790, and in little Sonoma that was enough to pay for the entire campaign for a candidate for public office.

A few days later I went to Tom and Jeri's for dinner.

"I've been *haunted* by the riverboat ride," Tom said. "The mirrors and the accordions! But those rich people loved it. I asked myself: *This* is our constituency?"

A couple of weeks later Dick Ashford held his own fund-raiser, and the two scenes provided an extraordinary contrast. Dick's venue was a large parabolic white tent at the Viansa Winery on a knoll with a panoramic view of nearly the entire Sonoma Valley. Viansa was as tacky in a pretentious middlebrow way as the *California Wine Ship* was tacky in a lowbrow way. Viansa was like a Las Vegas conception of a medieval Tuscan villa. It was adorned with newly painted frescoes executed in the trompe l'oeil style to appear as though they had been faded over the centuries. I had trouble believing that anyone's eye would really be fooled by the conceit. Inside there was an expansive store that sold dozens of types of mustards and olive oils and vinegars and prepared meals for gourmands for picnicking outside. Affluent tourists loved Viansa. The new-money crowd in Sonoma liked it, too. The bohemians knew that Alexis Gray held her wedding in that same tent, and that alone was enough to make them relentlessly suspicious of the place.

But Dick Ashford had shrewd reasons for selecting Viansa as his symbol. The owners were Vicky and Sam Sebastiani, who were a renegade branch of the greatest dynasty in Sonoma, a couple who had left the family's huge business, which sold mostly inexpensive wines, and started their own pricier boutique winery. (Viansa stood for *Vi*cky *an*d *Sa*m.) This way Dick showed his connection to Sonoma's old-money power structure and to the younger moneyed crowd all at once. Viansa had set aside one hundred acres as a wetlands ecological preserve, where Dick was a docent, so holding his fund-raiser there called attention to his environmentalism at the same time as it aligned him with the vintners and the free-market types.

I went to Dick's event along with Tom, Jeri, Ditty, and Gary, and they seemed dismayed to see so many prominent figures from the business community and even several key members of the Old Guard political machine. But they were especially shocked when, in the course of a seemingly endless speech during which he pointed out and thanked dozens of the people in attendance, Dick went over to Joe Costello and introduced Joe as his rival, not as his friend. That gesture convinced many of the bohemians that Dick was not their man. They only had Joe. But Dick's powerful display of his support at Viansa made it seem inevitable that he would win one of the two open chairs on the city council. The activists' hopes depended uneasily on Joe Costello defeating Jim Ghilotti.

AFTER THE FARMER'S MARKET on a Tuesday evening in August, I followed Tom Whitworth to a Craftsman cottage on the east side where the activists behind the Urban Growth Boundary were meeting in private to plan their campaign strategy.

We sat around the dining table as Tom showed off a print advertising campaign he had created with the tag line "Save Sonoma from Sprawl." He said that for his next propaganda stunt he wanted to give everyone "green belts"—quite literally, belts that went around the waistband of pants—as a way of illustrating the idea of preserving the greenbelt.

Larry Barnett was there in his informal capacity as a politically impassioned private citizen rather than in his official role as mayor of the town. Larry told the group that he had written a pro-UGB flyer aimed at the sizable population of the half-dozen mobile-home trailer parks on the west side.

"The residents don't like traffic," he said, "and they see the owners of the mobile parks as 'big business' and therefore bad."

They needed smart targeted advertising, Larry continued, especially since the editors of the *Index-Tribune*, which represented the business interests that were its advertisers, were using the newspaper as a "bully pulpit" against the UGB. Last week's paper had an editorial denouncing the RHI and UGB as NIMBYism. And this week's paper didn't have any letters in response, not even the one that Larry himself, the mayor, had sent in.

"We need seventy-five hundred bucks to run a good campaign," Larry said. They had already raised $1,000, and Wiley Hartman, a retired obstetrician-gynecologist who lived on the east side and spent most of his time working on his garden, had added $2,000 and promised $3,000 more as matching funds.

I lurked and listened, amazed to hear that one wealthy citizen could spend a mere $5,000 and his donation could be enough to decide an election that would determine the character and growth of the town for the next twenty years. Now it made even more sense to me why the locals were so afraid of the new-money invaders. If a small-time doctor could buy an election, what could a centimillionaire do?

Ken Brown arrived a half-hour late along with his young son, Moses, who was still wearing his soccer uniform. They had come directly from soccer practice.

I saw Ken and Larry together and wondered whether their combined presence was a violation of California's Brown Act. Tom had exposed illegalities when the Old Guard council members were meeting in private about Rosewood. Now, weren't the bohemian councilmen joining a private cabal to discuss town politics without informing the public? Wasn't this an illegal act of governmental secrecy? But I was a guest at the meeting and it didn't seem appropriate to point this out.

ON A WEDNESDAY NIGHT in September, the Sonoma Valley Citizens Advisory Committee held a public debate about the Urban Growth Boundary. Dick Ashford, hosting the gathering as a nonpartisan member of the committee rather than a candidate for city council, introduced the two teams of speakers.

Arguing against the UGB were Ditty Vella's father, Ig, whom Dick introduced to the audience as a "cheesemaker," and Art Fictenberg, a "real-estate developer." Arguing for the measure were the Mayor Larry Barnett and Dr. Wiley Hartman, whom Ashford said was an OB-GYN and the chairman of the town's planning commission and a "master gardener."

"I'd like to think that I'm a 'master cheesemaker!' " Ig Vella pro-
tested with a deadpan expression, evoking prolonged laughter. But
when the debates began, the overriding tone became serious and
sometimes outright combative.

"The quality of life we enjoy in Sonoma is a magnet attracting
developers with global reach," Larry said forcefully. "There wasn't
a telecommunications industry proposing 100,000-square-foot fa-
cilities near here ten years ago or corporations that control so much
wealth that they make most of the countries of the world look
poor. Sonoma may not have changed that much, but the world that
surrounds us has changed enormously. The UGB will prevent the
type of sprawl that ruined the Santa Clara Valley and much of California. Measure A last year was a perfect example of the power of
direct democracy. I'm glad whenever I see a public activated politically. This is against the trend in America. As mayor, when it
comes to land use, my hands are often tied. Sometimes government
is too slow or too unresponsive for the citizens to wait."

"The UGB will allow voters—*not* speculators, *not* developers,
not other interests—to decide," Wiley added. "Trust the voters as
we did with Rosewood."

"This isn't about fighting sprawl or wanting sprawl," countered
Art Fictenberg, who looked tough with his shiny bald head and a
goatee. "It's about *trust* in elected officials. I'm afraid the electorate
won't understand the issues or see the unintended consequences for
things other than their self-interest."

"I hope you're wrong," a woman from the audience interjected.
"I believe democracy works."

Ken Brown rose up and said indignantly and mockingly: "Mr.
Fictenberg, are you suggesting the average Sonoma citizen is uned-
ucated and will bite at a sound bite?"

"I counted seventy-two people here tonight," Ig Vella parried,
gesturing toward empty bleacher seats in the capacious civic auditorium attached to the Veterans Hall. "When we only fill seventy-

two of these chairs, I believe that you should think of *representative* democracy and not direct democracy."

Ig Vella's point stung for a while. But later, as I reflected on the scene, it impressed me that so many ordinary people had come out and engaged in a fervent discussion of fundamental issues of political philosophy. These people weren't lobbying city hall for petty grievances or financial gain; they were thinking far-sightedly about their community. I had worked for a summer in the White House and lived in New York and San Francisco, two highly politicized metropolises, but I hadn't heard anyone discussing these kind of underlying philosophical schisms since we studied the *Federalist Papers* in one of my undergraduate political science courses. I was very happy to be somewhere where ideas mattered.

THE THREE LEADING contenders for city council—Jim Ghilotti, Dick Ashford, and Joe Costello—had their first and only public confrontation in a Candidates Forum at the Sebastiani Theater, the old-time movie palace, on a Sunday afternoon. They took the stage along with four dark-horse entrants, including a retired grape grower who was conspicuous around town because, when the temperature was in the eighties, he wore well-tailored British dark-colored chalkstriped suits with Sartre-style silk cravats and when it was in the nineties he appeared in full safari-suit getups, in which, with his white beard and round belly, he looked like Ernest Hemingway in Africa.

The moderator asked about Sonoma's water shortage, which threatened to become a crisis before long. Sonoma's water for its drinking and plumbing needs came from the Russian River in the west of the county, and the Russian River drew water from the Eel River farther north amid the spectacular ancient redwood groves and marijuana farms of Humboldt County, where Julia "Butterfly" Hill had spent a year sitting atop a tree to protest logging practices.

The Eel River was terribly eroded. And so, the moderator asked, should Sonoma take more water from the Russian River? And if not, what were the alternatives? It was a blatantly divisive question.

Dick Ashford responded first with a strong plea for conservation and keeping Sonoma's land surfaces covered with earth that let rainwater seep down into the aquifer rather than sealing them with impenetrable asphalt and concrete.

"I'm putting my money where my mouth is," he said. "I tore up my yard, took out the driveway, and put in French drains. Turf is the biggest issue."

Joe Costello was ready with alarming figures about the crisis. "We draw eighty-four million gallons a day from the Russian River," he said. "The federal government is investigating the deprivation of salmon and trout, especially when the Eel River water is tunneled through the Russian River."

And then came Jim Ghilotti, and he was stolidly unrepentant.

"It's our water," he said flatly. "We paid for it."

Then the moderator asked about the Urban Growth Boundary, which the voter petitions had gotten placed on November's ballot as Measure S.

"Do you support it? What does an Urban Growth Boundary mean to you? And how will it hurt or hinder growth of affordable housing?"

Joe Costello said simply and unequivocally that he supported the UGB, but Ashford and Ghilotti waffled uncomfortably. Everyone knew from word of mouth that the idea might be too popular with voters for a candidate to oppose it officially, but nonetheless most politicians were palpably offended by ballot referendums that stripped their powers.

"I'm not publicly supporting or opposing Measure S," Ghilotti said. "Does it have any effect at all? No. Personally I think it's a feel-good measure."

"As a voter I'll vote no on S," Ashford said. "As a candidate I'm not campaigning either for or against Measure S. I believe in representative democracy and I've spent forty years of my life closely associated with *defending* representative democracy."

THE SUMMER WEATHER in the village of Sonoma was usually ideal—warm and dry, peaking in the low eighties—but for a few days in the middle of June 2000 it was uncharacteristically demonic. The *Index-Tribune* predicted a high of ninety-nine for Tuesday the thirteenth and 104 for Wednesday the fourteenth, readings that threatened to break the all-time records for these days. With forecasts of ninety-eight for Thursday and ninety-four for Friday, the townspeople readied for a languid week.

The delirious heat intensified the town's visions of impending doom. The omens were apocalyptic: The Empire News section of Tuesday's *Press-Democrat* led off with an article about the invasion of the "glassy-winged sharpshooter," the malicious insect that threatened to kill all the grapevines in Sonoma and Napa and swiftly devastate the wine business. The mysterious pest looked like a harmless tiny grasshopper, but the paper reported that the grape growers called it "the biggest threat in the history of California viticulture."

The insect infected vines with an incurable and fatal malady, a bacterial infection called Pierce's disease. The sharpshooter was native to the southeastern United States, but in such a tightly interlinked national economy, with huge commercial nurseries raising plants in Florida and Texas and shipping them to stores in other states, it was being transported inadvertently by truckers and then spreading its destruction in new places. I thought it was ironic that Gil Nickel from Far Niente owned exactly this kind of nursery in Texas. The success of the business in exporting houseplants to other states and regions was what had made his fortune and let him live the epitome of the elegant Napa Valley lifestyle. And now it was what might kill off his vines and reduce many tens of millions of dollars from the market value of his winery and his lands, especially the parcels he had recently purchased at a record-breaking $100,000 an acre.

In the past year the glassy-winged sharpshooter had wiped out vast acreages of vineyards in Southern California, and now it was moving northward through the great plains of the Central Valley. Sonoma and Napa were attempting to impose a "quarantine" by inspecting all deliveries of plants into the counties with a nearly fanatical vigilance. In May a batch of sharpshooter eggs was found in a Japanese aralia that had been sent from San Diego to the Home Depot near the northern reaches of the Sonoma Valley. And in early June, the newspaper reported, a second batch was found in another delivery of houseplants to a nursery just over Sonoma Mountain. Fortunately the local agriculture inspectors found the eggs. But if the creatures were able to hatch and get away, they could multiply and spread wildly through Sonoma and Napa and attack with the shocking suddenness, sweeping reach, and brutal power of a biblical plague. The wine country had to keep out the glassy-winged or suffer a catastrophe.

I had heard the local environmentalists talking about the sharpshooter for weeks. Many of them liked to gloat that the insect was nature's revenge on the overreaching greed and ambition of the grape growers and winemakers. They spoke of the sharpshooter as a righteous punishment for the vintners' foolishness in supplanting the richly diverse and harmonious ecosytems of the Sonoma and Napa valleys with a so-called monoculture. Now the valleys were unnecessarily vulnerable to infestation and predatory attacks because they depended entirely on a single crop. The environmentalists went around saying "nature abhors a monoculture." They claimed that the sharpshooter was nature's sly way of trying to restore the biological balance of a land that only a generation ago had as many fruit orchards and grazing ranches as vineyards. As the vintners pulled out the other breeds of trees and plants to make way for the most profitable cash crop, they invited this ecological disaster, the activists said. It was their comeuppance for having the hubris to undermine the natural order.

The sharpshooter might be defeated by a quarantine on imports of plants or by vigilant inspections at nurseries or, in the worst-case scenario, by an aerial spraying of pesticides over the county's farmlands. Already the Yes activists were very agitated and angry about the possibility of pesticide spraying. Gary Edwards sat on the Sonoma Valley Citizens Advisory Committee, which was supposed to be a voice for the people to the politicians on the county's board of supervisors, and he came back enraged from its meeting in early June, where he learned that Sonoma County was formulating plans for blanket preemptive spraying, so the poison would be in place to kill the bugs even before humans could detect them.

Gary had good reason for concern: Many Sonomans lived on or very close to the farms, and their own homes and gardens would be covered with toxic chemicals that could be harmful to people as well as to the pests. Another danger was that the sprays that killed sharpshooters would also eliminate many of the beneficial insects that kept nature in balance on organic farms and made pesticides unnecessary there. It would be several years before Sonoma's farmers could have their produce certified as "organic" again, since their lands would have been corrupted by chemicals. That would undermine the years of hard work and the idealistic ambitions of Bob Cannard, Jr., the Johnny Appleseed of Sonoma's environmental movement, and his many fervent followers and supporters—and threaten their livelihoods.

They were justly enraged.

Even with pesticide spraying, it was possible that the sharpshooters would repeatedly return to the vineyards, and that their recurring devastation would make it too costly for many winemakers to continually replant their vines, which took four or five years to grow to maturity. Eventually it could become uneconomical to grow wine grapes in Napa and Sonoma. In this scenario, the landowners would exert powerful pressures on the county government to change the zoning so that they could find a profitable use for their properties, such as putting up asphalt strip malls and tract housing subdivisions and corporate headquarters and new highways. This possibility, unthinkable until now, greatly increased the stakes around the Rural Heritage Initiative, which would limit the vineyards to agricultural use for thirty years.

I wanted to talk with some of the local farmers to see what they thought about the Rural Heritage Initiative and the glassy-winged sharpshooter. So I went to visit one of the biggest farmers in the Sonoma Valley and one of the smallest.

JIM BUNDSCHU didn't look like the scion of one of the oldest and most august families in the Sonoma Valley, the owner of three hundred acres of prime vineyards. He looked like an auto mechanic, both in his Everyman's facial features and his attire of workboots, old blue jeans covered with dirt and grass stains, and a green shirt—the kind of shirt that should have had a little horizontal oval on its breast saying "Jim" in linked cursive letters to identify him to customers.

He greeted me in the formal living room of the family's 1918 stone house in the Mayacamas foothills at the eastern edge of the Sonoma Valley. In both its rustic architecture and the surprising modesty of its size, the house reminded me of the home of the old Italian wine matriarch Sylvia Sebastiani. The stones had been quarried nearby when the land was cleared for farming. The living room interior showed continuity and reverence for older family. Glass cases held the kind of kitschy porcelain and ceramic figurines that were especially popular with well-to-do Germans in previous generations. The bookshelves had old editions of tomes on Sonoma history and novels by Jack London, who himself had been a farmer at the other end of this valley. The same architect had built the Bundschu house and Jack London's last house. A door opened onto a stone terrace with a barbecue and a bag of mesquite chips and containers of lighter fluid, but otherwise the decor suggested the parlor of an elderly grandmother. From the terrace we had a spectacular view of the great sweep of Bundschu vineyards and then the green floor of the Sonoma Valley and the mountains beyond.

Before we talked about the current issues, Jim told me the saga of his family's winery, Gundlach-Bundschu. They were the oldest family in the valley who were still vintners. The perils of the wine business had been devastating to several dynasties there. General Vallejo had a viticultural partnership with the Baron Haraszthy, but their heirs hadn't owned land in a long time. Even though Vallejo himself had twelve children, by the new millennium he had only one direct descendant, Martha McGettigan, and in recent years she had made a meager wage working behind the counter at the tasting room at another family's winery. The current scion of the Haraszthy clan was Vallejo Haraszthy, better known as Val. As a young man he had worked as a cellar rat at a winery along with Ken Brown. Haraszthy was paying $135-a-month rent on his house when he swapped leases for Brown's $45-a-month trailer. There were three other old wine dynasties still thriving in the Sonoma Valley—the Kundes, who had emigrated from Germany, and the Sebastianis and the Sangiacomos, from Italy—but the Bundschus were unusual in that they had been there since the 1850s, a half-century before the other great clans.

The patriarch Jacob Gundlach left Hamburg in 1849 and headed to California for the Gold Rush. He survived a shipwreck, made it to Sonoma after a full year of hard travel, and opened a brewery. Five years later he purchased hundreds of acres from Vallejo's son-in-law in one of the first legal handovers of title from the Spanish land grant. Gundlach named his property the Rhinefarm, and he traveled to Germany to marry and to bring back cuttings of vines to replant. Gundlach's daughter Francesca married Charles Bundschu, a fellow German immigrant. By the 1880s the family was making 180,000 cases of wine a year. The size of the business was astonishingly large for the era before the completion of the transcontinental railroad, when the wine had to be shipped down Sonoma Creek, through the Bay, and around South America to buyers on the East Coast.

The great 1906 earthquake and fire destroyed the family's warehouse in San Francisco. The workers tried to use the wine to put out the fire, which made it worse. Charles Bundschu never recovered psychologically from the loss, so Charles's son Walter took over. He shrewdly married an heiress named Sadie Towle, whose family had the money to refinance the business. But Sadie joined the Temperance movement. She wouldn't let them make wine. Nonetheless Walter kept growing grapes, which he sold to one of the biggest vintners in the Napa Valley, Inglenook, where his brother Carl became the winemaker. Walter's son Towle tore out half of the vines and used the land to grow pears and graze cattle.

Jim Bundschu was Towle's son, the clan's fifth generation, and he grew up on the family farm before attending the University of California at Berkeley from 1962 to 1966 during the period of student revolts and cultural upheaval.

"I was referred to as the token farmer," he said. "The land, if you have it in your soul, is a wonderful base in a time of social confusion. If you're close to nature you see both sides, the predator and the prey. At Berkeley I was a reed in the wind. I enjoyed Mario Savio"—the charismatic leader of the student protests—"but I also wanted to go to my history class."

When Jim graduated from Berkeley, he merged his instincts for commerce and his feel for nature by reviving the family's long-dormant viticulture business. Other Berkeleyites were "going back to the land" in a metaphorical sense, but Jim was doing it literally. He actually had land to go back to. In 1968 he replanted the grazing pastures with vines and signed a ten-year contract to sell grapes to the Sebastianis, who had a huge business selling cheap wines.

Jim became the protégé of the most powerful figure in the

Sonoma Valley in the twentieth century: August Sebastiani, who then was in his fifties. August sold a remarkable three million cases of wine a year before the advent of communications tools such as fax, e-mail, or Federal Express. He got up at four o'clock every morning to call his distributors in New York. Then August and Jim would meet for breakfast at four-thirty at the Lazy D (later renamed Ford's Café), a roadside diner amid the farms. The Lazy D didn't serve breakfast until five but they put out coffee at four. "If you weren't there by four-thirty you'd miss all the gossip," Jim recalled. "Who got into bar fights the night before. Who's going out with whom. Farming begins with the light, which comes around five-thirty in the summer." When wine writers visited from elite publications in New York, August wore overalls and took them to the Lazy D for a predawn breakfast and then at five A.M. he would drive them to his wetlands nature preserve and together they would feed his ducks. August was a great outdoorsman, and he took Jim to shoot the ducks and to fish for striped bass and sturgeon.

After two years of growing grapes for August Sebastiani, Jim decided to get into making and selling wine for his own label. "I wanted to bring wine to the common man instead of making it a snobby beverage," he said. "With my father, there was always wine at home and large dinners. We would see the fun and spirit of wine bringing people together, all the laughter around the table."

That was the family's saga. And so, as the Berkeley-educated sixties-generation inheritor of a 150-year dynasty, Jim Bundschu said that he was now trying to bridge the gap between the environmentalists and the grape growers.

"I've seen old pictures of the Rhinefarm with no trees in the background," he said. "The mountains were denuded because people used the trees for wood in the nineteenth century. There are more trees now than when Sonoma was first being settled. Grapes per se aren't the culprit. Humanity is."

I asked about the Town Hall Coalition's revolt against the vintners, which was triggered by Gallo razing stands of old-growth oaks, and their aspirations for restoring the vineyard lands back into small produce farms and dairies.

"Only one percent of the vineyards cut too many trees and planted the hillsides too steeply, but that led to a situation that will right itself again," he said. "The ambience of Sonoma's environment is totally dependent on vineyards because it's our last viable commercial crop. Every other product can be grown less expensively and with higher quality elsewhere. And Sonoma is a great place for people to live. Grapes are the only natural deterrent to that onslaught. Subdivisions and vineyards are worth about the same amount of money, so you can satisfy your greed by being a farmer. I don't care how ideological people are: Ninety-five percent of the future of Sonoma County and the Sonoma Valley is going to depend on maintaining a healthy vineyard business. And wine and good restaurants go hand-in-glove, that's why in the European wine country there are a lot of small truck farmers and little dairies and local cheesemakers. It's a more agrarian subculture, but it has to be driven by the wine business," which attracts the tourists who patronize the restaurants that support the small producers.

What about the Rural Heritage Initiative locking up the land for agriculture?

"I waffle on it," he said. "If Prohibition is declared again, or the vineyards are no longer viable because of an act of nature or God, there has to be some outlet to subsidize that, some alternative in case a disaster befalls the agriculture industry. What if the glassy-winged sharpshooter is devastating?

"There's an arrogance of trying to predict thirty years into the future. RHI erred because it doesn't leave an exit."

BY CONTRAST, Shelley Arrowsmith was one of the smallest farmers in the Sonoma Valley. She agreed to have me over to her little acreage, but since she was essentially a one-woman operation—her husband helped a bit—it was hard to find a time when she wasn't extraordinarily busy with her work. While we were waiting for a relatively slow period, I decided to search for more insights into the local farming culture by spending a day at the Sonoma County Fair.

When I arrived at the fairgrounds early on a Thursday morning in late July, I found that the day's first scheduled event was the lamb auction. The festivities were being held in a big barnlike structure with bleachers on the sides and a dirt floor. Many of the bidders wore woven Stetson-shaped hats. They ate the free doughnuts from a table beneath a large American flag. Some of the bidders sat in front of desktop calculators, ready for the action to begin.

At nine o'clock an announcer took the microphone and informed the "youngsters" to get ready at the livestock pen so they could bring their lambs to the stage when their lots were called. It seemed that all of the sellers were local teenagers from the Future Farmers of America or the 4H Club. They had raised the lambs themselves. I presumed that the point of this exercise was to show off the beauty of the animals, who would then return to the family farms as pets. But my naïve expectations were exploded when I read through the green-colored brochure from the front entrance table. The literature explained clearly that the auction was all about *meat*. None of the animals would leave here alive. They would be slaughtered and cut up and shipped as packaged food ready for storage in a freezer. The auction was all about teaching free-enterprise farming to kids. And the incentive was that the teens got to keep the money from the sales. The buyers were mostly the local supermarkets, which could charge extra for cuts from animals that had received prizes and ribbons in the County Fair. The windfalls were meant to encourage the teenagers to stay in Sonoma and work on farms rather than fleeing to the offices and service jobs in the urban centers.

Similar briberies took place throughout rural America, but it was even harder to retain the rising generation when they were so close to the decadent temptations of San Francisco and Silicon Valley—and, now, Telecom Valley.

"Let's sell some animals and have some fun!" the announcer boomed.

The national anthem was sung by a wholesome high school girl named Heather. The audience members all put their hands over their hearts as though they were grade-school students in small-town America in the 1950s. Heather's soprano voice struggled to pierce through the constant sound of baaahs. A chorus of lambs wailed from the pens behind the two auctioneers, who were elevated atop the large blocks of hay that served as a makeshift stage. A half-dozen teens were waiting in a row with their lambs lined up for sale and slaughter. The girls sported green kerchiefs tied in front and worn flat over the backs of their shoulders as though this were just another Girl Scouts outing.

Lot 1 was the fair's champion lamb, which had a banner draped over it as though it were Miss America. Its proud breeder and owner was Melanie, who was wearing the white jeans and neat blue sweatshirt of the Future Farmers of America.

The bidding started at $10 and went up rapidly in $1 increments as a row of teenage girls clapped rhythmically in unison. There was a big uproar from the crowd at $26 and again at $30. The audience was exuberant—clapping, jumping, acting as though this were pro sports. Finally the animal sold for $41 to J & G Market, and a photographer appeared to shoot the girl with her doomed lamb, a final picture before the creature was turned into chops and loins and shanks.

For Lot 2, the girl struggled to keep the lamb's head still by cradling it with motherly affection between her arm and shoulder. The lamb sold for $21.

Then came a very tall boy who held his lamb's head dangerously close to his crotch. The boy wore the white shirt and green tie of the 4H uniform. His Lot 3 sold for $18 to Food for Less, and then 4 went for $16 to Safeway.

The winning bids seemed incredibly cheap to me until I looked in the green brochure and saw that the auction's quoted dollar prices were per pound of flesh. It was if Christie's and Sotheby's sold Picassos by the square inch.

Outside the lamb barn, thousands were enjoying their cotton candy and snow cones and candied apples and popcorn and lemonade and corn dogs and corn on the cob and fudge. They flocked to the instant photo booths and the pony rides and the free seminars on how to bet on the horses in that afternoon's thoroughbred races. They gaped at a hall of prize-winning flowers that had a big banner saying "FLASH GARDEN: To boldly grow where no flower has grown before." The musical theme from *Star Wars* was playing from the loudspeaker. Flying saucers hung from the hall's ceiling. An exhibit showed a Martian happily drinking a bottle of wine.

I wasn't interested in returning to the livestock barn for the auctions of the rabbits and the pigs and the cattle and the chickens. As I walked around the fairgrounds, I looked once again through my brochures and found a section entitled "Facts about Sheep." It explained that the average sheep can have a productive life of seven years, but many young sheep—better known as lambs—were killed when they reached a "market weight" of 90 to 115 pounds after being alive for only five months. I did some quick mental calculations and figured that those smiley teenagers in their white outfits were taking home $1,500 to $5,000 apiece for just a few months of work. The catch was that they had to kill off a cute pet many years before its time. It seemed like a forbiddingly Faustian bargain to present to an idealistic sixteen-year-old kid. And if Sonoma, like farm communities everywhere, had to bribe its best high-school students to try to get them to stay on the farms, I didn't believe that the Rural Heritage Initiative had much of a chance.

This idea was further confirmed as I drove through the farmlands on the way back to the town of Sonoma. Almost everywhere I saw signs saying "Save Our Farms—No on I." They were part of the farm lobby's disinformation campaign. They were spreading the Big Lie, repeated so often that it seemed to be true, that RHI (also known as Measure I) would stop farmers from taking a corner of the family's ranch and building a second house there for their grown children, thus forcing the rising generations to leave the land. This wasn't true—RHI did nothing to change the old rules, which allowed one additional dwelling for the farmer's immediate family as well as detached housing for the farmworkers and attached "granny units" in many places. But the advertising campaign was pervasive, and people were starting to believe it.

WHEN I ARRIVED at Arrowsmith Farm on a weekday morning in early August, I walked around and found Shelley Arrowsmith's husband, Norm, feeding their chickens. He threw them large sections of papayas and watermelons with the outer skins still attached, ears of corn on the cob, entire zucchinis, and a prodigious amount of mesclun salad greens. I looked on, thinking that these frenzied birds were consuming more servings of healthy fruits and vegetables at this one feeding than most Americans would on a typical day. I was even more astonished when Norm said that this food came from the most expensive supermarket in town, the Sonoma Market, where the affluent east side crowd shopped. The market needed to maintain a reputation for peak ripeness to justify its high prices, so it wouldn't sell its organic salad mix for more than a single day, he explained. The next morning Shelley or Norm would come by and pick up the inevitable leftovers—which were still fairly fresh—and feed them to their remarkably fortunate birds. The hens seemed outrageously happy.

Shelley appeared and the three of us sat down to share sourdough bread and preserves at a little table beneath a trellis covered by wild grapevines. I tried to appear comfortable despite the constant and unnerving presence of swirling bumblebees—Norm raised hundreds of bees and Shelley sold their honey and wax—and the occasional distractions of the rambunctious chickens, which walked up to us as though they were household pets to demand attention. These were truly "free-range" chickens. They seemed to have a license to wander nearly everywhere throughout the two and a half acres of the property.

Shelley and Norm were environmental activists from the city, and the farm was their admirable effort to walk the walk rather than just talking the talk. Norm was an architect and land-use planner who had lived in England and continental Europe before coming to San Francisco and founding the Institute for the Human Environment in 1972. Shelley was an environmental designer who had lived in Marin County, in Sausalito, an old fishing village turned upscale suburb. Together they ran Norm's nonprofit and struggled to protect nature in places as far-flung as Sweden, Alaska, the Mediterranean, Samoa, China, and Hawaii. After two decades of this work, they saw an opportunity to take individual action by buying a small farm while they could still afford one.

They came to Carneros, the region that spanned the southern reaches of both Napa and Sonoma counties. Carneros was Spanish for "sheep," and the name had been fitting for most of the century, when nearly the entire area was dry grazing land. The radical change came in the early nineties, when Sonoma's planners began interesting the Carneros farmers in taking the wastewater from the towns. The sewage from the village of Sonoma became the irrigation source for a rapid proliferation of vineyards. And now Carneros was mostly covered with vines. The area's microclimate turned out to be extraordinarily well-suited for growing chardonnay and pinot noir, the grapes that blend into champagne. Carneros was only a few miles away from the centers of the Napa and Sonoma valleys, but on a summer day Carneros might be as much as ten degrees cooler because it was closer to San Francisco Bay and more openly exposed to the fog and winds. While cabernet sauvignon grew extremely well in the hotter valley cores, the champagne grapes took best to the cooler places. And so Taittinger, the last great family-owned French Champagne dynasty, had bought vineyards nearby and built an ersatz replica of the clan's eighteenth-century château in Epernay.

But Carneros still had a honky-tonk little enclave of two-and-a-half-acre farms that had been subdivided out of a large chicken farm way back in 1912. That's where Shelley and Norm were able to obtain their humble plot seven years ago.

They bought naked land that had been trampled by horses for so long that it wouldn't grow anything. For income they rented out three of the four tiny cottages on the property, creating a bohemian community along with a Berkeley professor, a nurse, and a sculptor who worked in alabaster.

They had to spend a couple of years just building up the soil so it would be rich enough for farming. Shelley went to Bobby Cannard for mentoring. He told her to plant cover crops to hold down the soil from the winds that swept through the open plain. For an organic fertilizer she bought pigeon manure from a neighbor who raised squab for Alice Waters at Chez Panisse. Bobby introduced her to a nursery that wanted to hold a pumpkin festival, so she chose pumpkins as her first crop. And at Bobby's suggestion she made a compost pile with alfalfa, straw, rock dust, and oyster shells. Unfortunately, the pile was the perfect moist place for snails and slugs, which feed on plants and leave trails of slimy mucous. Shelley found herself patrolling the farm at midnight with a flashlight, and when she saw a slug she would sprinkle salt on it, but the creatures shook off the salt and survived. Shelley became desperate to find some way to kill them without applying chemicals. So a neighboring farmer sold her two chickens and two ducks. The birds sucked up bugs as though they were vacuum cleaners. Another neighbor arranged for Shelley to supply eggs to Babbette's, the fanciest restaurant in the town, and before long she was raising nineteen chickens and nineteen ducks and selling the extra eggs herself at the farmer's market the same day that they were laid.

Shelley began growing baby arugula and watercress for Babette's and several other expensive restaurants in town. Her reputation was so good that one of the prestigious chefs began naming "Arrowsmith Farms" on his menu as the source of his greens. Shelley actually farmed only one of their acres, proving it was possible to survive financially if you made high-quality niche products and worked extremely hard.

Shelley and Norm were perhaps the smallest commercial farmers in Sonoma. I wanted to know what they thought about the political controversies.

"The economics of the vineyards are driving the environment of the whole place," Norm said. "A century ago farmers planted eucalyptus trees here. Now vineyards are chopping them down so they can plant vines right up to the property boundary. But you lose the windbreaks. The old farmers knew better."

"This area has a problem with the sharpshooters and Pierce's disease because it's a monoculture," Shelley said. "There's nothing else growing here that harbors the beneficial insects that would fight Pierce's disease. Even though the vineyards tend to farm organically, it's not a balanced ecosystem. A lot of the problems with pests and diseases are because you don't have the balance anymore."

What about the Rural Heritage Initiative and Urban Growth Boundary?

"I see so many different sides to it," Shelley said cautiously. "It's not as simple as people are making it out to be. People haven't looked at it from a *whole* perspective. Where will it push development?"

Norm suggested that one way to look at RHI was by studying Napa's agricultural preserve. "It's hard to live on your own farm in Napa because the policy is not to have residences or businesses that support farms. The idea is to live in the towns. That's not how it is in France or some of the places we admire where you have your own land, you protect it, you don't work only nine to five."

Listening to Shelley and Norm, I was further convinced that the Rural Heritage Initiative wasn't going to pass.

To lighten the conversation I mentioned my experience at the lamb auction at the county fair and my surprise that the prize-winning animals would be slaughtered soon after they had their photos taken along with the teenagers.

"Our problem," Shelley confessed, "is that we weren't raised as farmers, so we can't bring ourselves to kill our chickens."

One of the free-range birds walked by, and I looked at it, thinking how lucky it was that it could eat salad greens and papaya for the rest of its long life.

Back in the village I told Ditty Vella, a forceful advocate of RHI, that Shelley seemed to oppose the measure.

"Shelley Arrowsmith has an unrealistic view," Ditty snapped back. "She's from suburban Marin and she's living out her fantasy of having a dream farm."

FOUR SEASONS coincided from April through November: in climate, the dry season, when it hardly rained; in the economy, the tourist season, when seemingly every weekend there was an outdoor festival or event; in the wine business, the growing season, when the grapes were tended, ripened, harvested, and crushed; and in politics, the campaign season, culminating in the election. So the many public debates on issues had to compete for attention with various happenings that became more ridiculous and sublime as the summer passed.

The craziness began most earnestly on the Fourth of July in Kenwood, a hamlet in the northern reaches of the Sonoma Valley, which held what it billed as the World Championship Pillowfights. In each brief bout the two contestants straddled a long pole above a deep puddle of mud. Then they whacked each other on the head and torso with oversized wet pillows until one was knocked into the pit. For the male contestants—hunky firefighters and construction workers who stripped off their shirts—the event was mainly a chance to display their musculature to a crowd of hundreds of admiring girls. The female contestants seemed divided into tomboys who liked the vicious mudslinging aspect and sixteen-year-olds eager to show off their figures in wet T-shirts.

The pillowfights initiated the summer into weekends of grape-stomping contests for the locals and water-hose fights between the valley's rival volunteer fire departments. The farmer's market, struggling to attract buyers for gorgeous tomatoes and eggplants when most residents couldn't give away the surplus ones that they grew themselves, sparked more interest with an edible art sculpture contest and with races of ripe zucchinis turned into model cars. Brad Gross's daughter and many other fearless children went into the woods to practice the flying trapeze with a professional troupe. Tobias Weinberger, the son of the couple who owned Readers' Books, covered his outstretched arms with firecrackers and set them off on stage as part of Oddville, a cross between a circus sideshow, vaudeville, and avant-garde performance art. Jim Bundschu wore a chicken suit to the Sonoma Valley Wine Auction, where the movie animator John Lasseter literally sold the shirt off his back to raise money for charity.

But the show to outdo all shows turned out to be a public forum held in September, as the harvest was beginning, by the Town Hall Coalition, the environmental activist group that opposed the spraying of pesticides in the vineyards both as a routine practice every year—a task assigned to migrant workers, who might be harmed by the repeated exposures—and as a hasty emergency precaution, an aerial assault against the invasion of the glassy-winged sharpshooter.

A couple of days before the pesticide protest, I saw Ditty Vella at the farmer's market. She was volunteering at a small table where several Yes Group activists were handing out campaign buttons and flyers for Joe Costello's city council bid and talking about his platform. I asked Ditty whether she would be attending the Town Hall meeting.

"I can't bear to go even though my ex-husband is a speaker," she said. "Even though I agree with them, those people make me embarrassed to be an environmentalist because they're so dogmatic and strident."

With my expectations prepared accordingly, I showed up at the event, which filled a large hall at the parish house of the local Congregational church. The walls were covered with poster-sized propaganda photos with provocative headlines. One picture showed a child with ugly red marks on his face, presumably from reactions to toxins spayed near where he lived. "Is your wine worth this?" read the tag line.

Another blown-up black-and-white photograph depicted a tractor spraying mists of chemicals: "Morning in romantic Sonoma Valley."

A prop plane dumping a trail of toxins on the fields: "A romantic (pesticide-slathered) Napa." A closer shot of the drifts of noxious chemicals carried aloft by strong winds: "Sonoma and Napa: A glass of wine with your illness?"

Before the formal program began I came across Lynn Hamilton, the founder of the Town Hall Coalition, a healthy outdoors type who looked fortysomething. She seemed more like a soccer mom than a radical feared by the establishment.

"Growing up in the western side of the county, I always thought the vineyards in Sonoma Valley were great," she said. "It wasn't until the vineyards started coming to west county and cutting down thousand-year-old redwoods that we became alarmed."

The panel of speakers was introduced by mayor Larry Barnett. He was wearing what he usually wore to city council meetings—a white dress shirt and a conservative necktie—and his cheeks appeared particularly full and ruddy. Facing that crowd Larry looked like the old robber-baron J. P. Morgan transported by time machine to an Earth First convention. But as soon as Larry began making his fervent speeches, he displayed an ideological passion rare among politicians.

"When the question is posed whether we need to balance economic interests versus the public interest, I'm astonished that the conversation is even taking place," he said. "Vineyards and agriculture in Sonoma are undergoing the same corporatization phenomenon as other industries. There's no question that corporate agriculture is addicted to chemicals and pesticides. We can't perform a controlled experiment on the human race but we are doing that. We are the guinea pigs."

The evening's featured speaker was Marc Lappe, who had received a Ph.D. in pathology from the University of Pennsylvania and done postdoctoral cancer research at the University of California at Berkeley before founding the Center for Ethics and Toxics in a tiny village on the Pacific coast. He had come to discuss the glassy-winged sharpshooter.

"This is not an emergency *health* situation," he said emphatically. "This is an emergency *dollar* situation. You don't have to take the brunt for someone else's economic risk taking. There's no such thing as a wine-grape emergency. Nobody is going to die. But somebody *is* going to die if we use pesticides!"

The applause lasted for a long time.

"I'm dismayed that in our culture we're making decisions between profits and health," Larry Barnett said. "Corporations would like you to think of democracy as Americans' freedom to go to the mall and pick out colors. You're going to have to overcome your apathy. You're going to have to overcome your disillusionment and get involved in politics."

"I have an objection to the word *pest*," said Ditty Vella's exhusband, the organic farmer Bobby Cannard, who had long, unruly black hair peppered with gray and white. He spoke in a squeaky voice reminiscent of the late comedian Andy Kaufman from "Taxi" and "Saturday Night Live." To this crowd he was akin to a revered guru. He had personally inspired many of them.

"Bugs are an indicator of health," he continued. "That bug that comes along and makes me sick is telling me that I've stepped over my consumptive bounds." In other words, the glassy-winged sharpshooter was nature's revenge on greed.

"The luxury wine industry's monoculture is the problem," said another organic farmer. "If it's not this bug, it will be another."

"When you create a huge food supply in the natural world, something comes along to eat it," said a clean-cut youthful environmentalist who carried a Palm Pilot.

"Quarantine won't work," said Bobby Cannard. "The bug will get here. The only thing that will work is biodiversity and environmental health. Biologically sound agriculture was the only agriculture until the petrochemical industry needed an outlet for their products after World War II."

"The pesticide industry is the result of the industrial revolution that has run its course," said a slender hippie chick with beautiful long straight blonde hair.

"We're ready to create a boycott of California wine!" someone exclaimed. The audience erupted with applause.

"Tens of millions of dollars are being spent on corporate welfare," said Larry Barnett. "Why don't they raise the price of their chardonnay by two dollars a bottle and not burden the taxpayers?" There was even more applause.

"Most of the 'small farmers' I have near me are Intel Corporation people," said a thin silver-haired woman. "They've bought a hundred acres and they are building big houses and trophy vineyards and the 'vineyard managers' are former mechanics who don't know what's what."

"It seems that this comes down to whether the right of the wine industry to make a profit supersedes the rights of individuals to health and welfare," said Will Shonbrun. "Is the value of grapes higher than the health of people? Let's show these folks what democracy really means and have it bite them in the you-know-what."

VOTER TURNOUT was remarkably high in the town of Sonoma even during normal years, but for the fervently anticipated November 2000 election, when so much about the place's future was at stake, the mobilization was an extraordinary eighty-four percent: 5,105 of the 6,079 registered voters cast their ballots. Some of the candidates and many of the local political enthusiasts spent the evening of Tuesday November 7 drinking beer at Murphy's Irish Pub and waiting for the returns, but there were so many absentee ballots—people weren't going to miss this election even if they were traveling—that the final results weren't clear for several days. When the count was finished and certified, the outcomes were unexpected.

Although an editorial in the Sonoma *Index-Tribune* had endorsed Dick Ashford and Jim Ghilotti for the city council, praising Ghilotti as "a down-to-earth, common-sense guy," neither man was the top vote-getter. The leading choice of Sonoma's citizens was the candidate of the Yes Group of activists, Joe Costello, whose 2,272 votes equaled 26.9 percent of the total. (Voters marked their ballots for two candidates to fill the two opening seats, so fifty percent was the highest possible result for any contender.) Dick Ashford was the runner-up with 1,829 votes for a 21.7 percent share, clinching the second of the chairs.

The *Index-Tribune* had opposed the Urban Growth Boundary, but the citizens approved it overwhelmingly with 63.7 percent of the vote. Sonoma wouldn't grow past its current tightly conscribed borders for another twenty years. Two and a quarter square miles— that was all. There would be no new Armstrong Estates, no monstrous trophy houses clustered on small lots replacing the greenbelt of farmland around the town.

The bohemians' big defeat was the Rural Heritage Initiative, which fell short by seven percent of the vote. The disinformation campaign by the farm lobby had succeeded. Farmers believed the false claim that RHI would stop them from building a second house for their grown children to live in on the family ranch. And even when they grasped the facts, their dirty secret was that they didn't want to be stuck farming for the next thirty years when perhaps they could sell out to a developer and not have to get up at four in the morning anymore. The problem with the bohemian dream of a rural paradise was getting someone in twenty-first-century America to continue the agrarian grind of the nineteenth. There were a few leaders like Bobby Cannard and a few idealistic followers like Shelley Arrowsmith and her husband, Norm, but there weren't enough. The bohemians idealized the shitkickers, but maybe those noble shitkickers were just tired of kicking the shit.

The failure of RHI meant that most of Sonoma County was vulnerable to development, but the UGB's passage ensured that the Sonoma Valley was safe. It was only a small corner of a very large county, but still that was a real victory. For the bohemians, it was their own little realm. They were guilty of NIMBYism—they had proclaimed "not in my backyard!"—but it was hard for me to see this as anything other than a triumph.

At the next city council meeting, Joe Costello and Dick Ashford took their oaths for four-year terms of office. "First you're sworn in," one of the two departing Old Guard members warned them, "and then you're sworn at."

The newly reconstituted council's first official action was to vote five to nothing to select Ken Brown as the new mayor and Joe Costello as the vice-mayor. They joined Larry Barnett, who remained on the council, in an unbreakable three-member majority for the activists.

The bohemians had taken over city hall.

In the coming months they asserted their power vigorously. They voted a moratorium on the construction of new hotels, preventing Rosewood or other developers from trying to come back to the town. They approved plans for "affordable housing" so the natives would still be able to live there. And they blocked a previously approved proposal for Lofts Unlimited to put "live-work lofts" near the Plaza. The company was infamous in San Francisco for erecting ugly hulking buildings in bohemian neighborhoods. The lofts were supposed to be for artists who needed large spaces, but were inevitably colonized by wealthy professionals instead. Ditty Vella spoke at a city council meeting and opposed the expensive loft condos because firemen, nurses, and teachers couldn't afford to live there. It didn't help the developers that their front man in Sonoma had pled guilty to bank fraud charges only a few years earlier. Larry Barnett had fought them bitterly before the November election, but the Old Guard had approved the construction nonetheless. Now that the Old Guard was out, the bohemians killed the lofts.

Ken Brown exulted in his role as mayor, a spectacular transformation for a guy who had come to the valley a quarter-century earlier and found work there as a grape picker and a cellar rat. He decided that he needed to confer with the other men named Brown who were also mayors of Bay Area cities. And so the new mayor of Sonoma (pop. 9,000) went to Oakland (pop. 450,000) for a tête-à-tête with the national liberal icon Jerry Brown, and he took Tom Whitworth with him to the imposing neoclassical city hall in San Francisco (pop. 800,000) to schmooze the machine politician Willie Brown, who was under federal investigation for alleged corruption. Ken brought a large wheel of Vella cheese and a bottle of organic wine with him. Willie Brown greeted him effusively, and as they posed together for the photo opportunity, Willie paused to pick up the cheese and wine, saying: "Let's make sure to get the bribes in the picture!"

The Sonoma Hillside Preservation Alliance, a.k.a. the Yes Group, succeeded in building a hiking trail on the hillside behind the cemetery. Jeri Lynn helped organize teams of dozens of volunteers who got down on their knees and pulled out prodigious amounts of poison oak. The state of California agreed to pay most of the costs of cleaning up the toxic old dump site nearby. The trail was completed in August 2001, and it quickly became beloved by Sonoma's residents.

The conspicuous loser of the city council race was Jim Ghilotti, who suffered a particularly humiliating defeat. Ghilotti had lavished an unprecedented $19,000 on his campaign, which was more than ten times as much as Joe Costello had raised with his tacky riverboat cruise and nearly four times as much as Ken Brown had spent on his own winning race two years earlier. Ghilotti's expenditures were considered so excessive given Sonoma's small population and geographic size that the city council passed new limits on campaign contributions (of $100 per voter) and advocated a $10,000 ceiling for total outlays by each candidate.

Ghilotti's close friends and neighbors said that he didn't have the same spirit after losing the election. They said that the pressures of public life had been difficult for the building contractor. But no one foresaw what he might do.

On Wednesday, May 20, 2001, sometime between noon and one, Ghilotti was seen praying at St. John Chrysostom, a large Catholic church in the working-class Inglewood neighborhood of Los Angeles. There was no explanation for his presence there. He hadn't told his family or colleagues that he would be traveling, and he didn't have business dealings in southern California. The church was only about a mile away from the Los Angeles International Airport. A janitor saw Ghilotti alone in the chapel. Ghilotti was dressed entirely in black.

At one-thirty a woman noticed Ghilotti's body slumped life-lessly over the steering wheel of a Chevrolet Silverado truck in the church's crowded parking lot. She called for paramedics, who arrived within minutes.

The truck's doors were locked. A discharged gun was found inside.

James J. Ghilotti was pronounced dead at 1:37 P.M.

He was forty-six years old.

There was luggage in the truck, but no suicide note was found. The coroner announced the cause of death as a "self-inflicted gun-shot to the head."

The news horrified Ghilotti's hometown. Even his political op-ponents, who had taken such delight in their rivalry, were melan-choly and bewildered. They had despised Ghilotti's positions, but they never wished him harm. They had never really known him. Even though Sonoma was a small town, small enough for nearly everyone to know everyone else who got involved in the commu-nity, the two sides were so insular and divided that the leaders of the bohemians and the leaders of the business interests rarely con-nected as people.

The town buzzed with talk about possible motivations for the suicide. The *Index-Tribune*, ever respectful in its old-fashioned way, shrank from speculation, but the countywide *Press-Democrat*, which was owned by the *New York Times*, responded with sharp inves-tigative reporting. The paper revealed that Ghilotti had testified before a grand jury in a federal investigation of corruption in the Bay Area municipality of Richmond, where the local officials had allegedly demanded bribes in exchange for city contracts. Ghilotti told friends that he was a whistleblower and had worn a wire to help the FBI. He even talked about making a payoff on a Sausalito boat as part of a sting operation.

But some people in Sonoma remained skeptical of the idea of Ghilotti as an undercover crusader. After all, Ghilotti's firm had received contracts from the city of Richmond. And what contractor ever wore a wire for the feds unless they had pinched him first? And why would he become a canary when he was about to take over as head of the builders' lobbying association for the entire north coast? And if he were one of the good guys, then why had he killed himself? The more plausible reasons seemed to be real culpability combined with the one-two punch of embarrassing political defeats—first his failed lobbying for a widening of Highway 101 through the center of Sonoma County, and then his defeat in his own small hometown.

To people in the outside world, the travails of a village with only two-and-a-quarter square miles and a few thousand inhabitants might not seem so important in the overall scheme. But to the insiders it *was* their world. And in such a small place with such a strong sense of community, isolated by its mountainous geography and by the insular attitudes of its populace, the scrutiny of the neighbors created a constant visibility and a relentless pressure. It was easy to reinvent yourself and find a new social scene within San Francisco or Los Angeles or New York, but not in Sonoma. Community was a fading ideal in America and it was worth fighting for, as the Sonoma activists had done, but it also had a darker side.

One season of Sonoma politics had exhausted me. After the 2000 election I gave up my Kato Kaelin houseguest routine and resumed my previous life in San Francisco, where my girlfriend, Katharine, and I shared an apartment of our own. As much as I had loved staying in Sonoma, it was refreshing to get back to the city, where I could walk through a dozen neighborhoods without worrying that my friends would accost me and regale me with their latest political animosities.

I came back occasionally for Thursday night dinners at Tom and Jeri's and for Tuesday farmer's markets and for Celia and David's summer weekend parties at their east side cottage. But I sensed that some of the bohemians, Ditty and Gary especially, felt my distance was a personal affront, as if by returning to the city I had rejected the club they had let me into. By leaving Sonoma I wasn't just following my own life's path, but rejecting theirs, or so they made me feel. When I saw them at Celia's parties they didn't receive me with the same effusiveness and warmth as before. I again considered moving to Sonoma to stay but realized that I only knew one person there between the ages of nineteen (Emma, who worked at the bookstore and painted sets for Oddville) and forty-one (Jeri Lynn). Sonoma was one of the best possible places to raise a family or retire, but singles and childless couples in their twenties and thirties would seek out the economic opportunity, diversity, and stimulation of a major city. If Sonomans wanted young, well-educated people to add a different element to the life of the town, maybe they should have allowed construction on new apartments for commuters from the Telecom Valley over the hill. The village had become so polarized by its political feuds that the advocates of a middle road of carefully balanced growth ultimately had little chance to prevail.

But there were a few signs of reconciliation and greater understanding. I was surprised when Ditty and Gary developed a real friendship with Celia and David who, after all, were rich invading weekend people from Silicon Valley, which was exactly what the activists had renounced and fought. Early on there were some tensions. Ditty had chafed when Celia only told her on a Friday about a Sunday party, as though it were an afterthought and Ditty weren't really good enough for Celia and her fancy friends visiting from the city. But Celia and David became quite close with Brad and Sue Gross across the street. And Sue was Gary's sister. Gary and David shared an entrepreneurial streak. The clincher to their friendship came when Gary convinced David to invest with him in a dairy farm in Oregon that produced cow's milk for cheeses. David enthusiastically bought four cows for $10,000 apiece and he liked driving ten hours north through the boondocks to visit the animals. Even Celia seemed startled that David had bought *cows*. But as Internet and technology stocks were collapsing, cows seemed like a safe, shrewd investment. Once David and Gary were business partners, the two couples became even closer. My city friends had gone native in Sonoma. Still, Ditty stubbornly resisted when Celia and David asked her repeatedly to join them in buying Italian Vespa scooters in a trio of coordinated colors—a red, a white, and a blue—so they could drive together as a patriotic display in the Fourth of July parade at the Plaza.

AFTER FOUR YEARS of cohabitation, Tom Whitworth and Jeri Lynn Chandler decided to get married in April 2001. Ken Brown performed the honors at city hall. The couple wanted the ceremony to be extremely low-key so the only person they invited was Ditty's son Marius, who would take the photographs. But later that day they threw a very casual reception at their loft for the Sonoma bohemians. I came to congratulate them and to taste Tom's new vintage of homemade wine, which was absolutely awful. I found myself talking with Marius's father, Bobby Cannard, Jr. I told him that the previous night Katharine had taken me to the Chez Panisse Café in Berkeley for my birthday and we ordered a salad of romaine that was identified as coming from his Cannard Farm. Katharine had said it was surely the best salad she ever had. The leaves were small tender curled balls rather than the usual large sheets of greens in a classic Caesar. Bobby replied that he didn't know why the restaurant couldn't get it right, but what we had eaten was actually a species of French butter lettuce rather than a romaine. That reassured me that Sonoma was still even more Berkeley than Berkeley.

THE CRASH of the NASDAQ stock market in the first three months of 2001 slowed the new-money invasion temporarily. The paper worth of many plutocrats was decimated, but nonetheless they still had their houses and lands in the wine country. It was as if, at precisely the right time, they had followed the advice from *Gone With the Wind* when the plantation owner Gerald O'Hara told his daughter: "The land, Katie Scarlett! The land is what matters! The land is what lasts!"

In the summer of 2001, after a year and a half of planning and construction, my friend Marc Benioff finally completed the remodeling of his mansion near the top of a mountain overlooking the Napa Valley. When Katharine and I came to visit on a weekend afternoon, we wandered into the unlocked kitchen and found a very tall and slender woman with brown hair who looked as though she could appear in a Ralph Lauren clothing ad in *Vanity Fair*.

"I'm Lynn," she said.

Even after the crash, techno-moguls still had spectacular country houses and remarkable girlfriends. Lynn worked for the public-relations firm that I had advised Marc to hire, so indirectly I was responsible for their liaison. Marc had offered me some stock options as a thank-you for introducing and recommending him to the firm, so now I wondered whether I were also something of an accidental procurer.

Marc took us through the living room, which now had expansive windows and a magnificent view where there used to be a plastered wall. But other than passing by on the way to and from the kitchen, none of us spent any time in that room, which made Marc's feat of engineering seem rather unnecessary. It was hard to believe that anyone would linger inside a house that had such an incredible pool. Seen from above, the pool's elliptical curve resembled the wing of a bird. It was an infinity pool, meaning that the far edge didn't have a railing or lip; the water fell sharply at a ninety-degree angle as if it were a sculptural waterfall. The effect was hypnotic. The pool was extraordinarily large: one hundred feet by forty feet. Many pools at major luxury resort hotels weren't as large or elegant. Marc had spent about a million dollars on the pool, and all the money showed. Katharine, a swimming champ in her school days, dove in and swam laps.

"This is the nicest pool I've ever swam in," she declared.

Katharine liked it so much she swam a mile while Marc and I talked in the hot tub. He complained about the ludicrous cost overruns and about how the contractors in Napa ran a notorious racket and about the prohibitive expenses of heating such an enormous volume of water. I asked why he hadn't built the pool house he had commissioned from Larry Ellison's modernist architect, Olle Lundberg. The pool house itself was supposed to be worthy of appearing in an architectural magazine. It was designed to have an indoor-outdoor fireplace, a loft bedroom, and a kitchen.

"I decided not to throw away another million dollars," Marc said.

I didn't see Marc for another several months, but when I received the invitation to his Christmas party, I figured that he must be feeling richer once again. As he had done before the crash, Marc rented out an entire restaurant downtown: Roy's, the swank San Francisco outpost of one of Hawaii's celebrity chefs. As before, Marc hired a troupe of Hawaiian drummers and hula dancers to perform, and he served seemingly limitless amounts of the finest sushi and seared fish. But when I told him that I wanted to swim with him in Napa again, Marc confessed that he had sold the house soon after the terrorist attacks of September 11 because he had feared lasting repercussions in the real-estate market.

I wondered how many other new-money invaders were retreating from the wine country. As one way of measuring, I called on Marc's architect, Olle Lundberg, in the spring of 2002. Olle was one of the top architects working in the Napa Valley, where he had completed twenty houses. But Olle himself was more of a bohemian in the mold of Sonoma County, where he kept his own weekend retreat near the coastline.

Olle's studio was in a San Francisco warehouse district called Dogpatch, near the badlands of the docks. The neighborhood was just starting to gentrify. His location might have been dangerous if a Hell's Angels clubhouse weren't next door. Olle worked out of a stunningly expansive space. We met in a loft conference room that looked down on one side at the desks of a half-dozen young design assistants and on the other at an industrial workshop where Olle liked to drive the forklift and supervise the fabrication of parts of his buildings. "I like using the process of manufacturing to intensify the design," he said. "We'll build the 'signature pieces.' The front door. The toilet paper holder."

Olle was a big guy, well over six foot tall with the broad build of a Nordic longshoreman. But he wore his long hair tied back in a ponytail, which made him look more like an urban avant-garde artist or at least a renegade country rock and roller. He had grown up in the South and studied sculpture and English literature at Washington and Lee University, where he was the editor of the literary magazine, a role that the renowned writer Tom Wolfe had held years earlier. Realizing that his visual artistry felt more natural than his prose efforts, he studied architecture at the University of Virginia and later established his firm in San Francisco. He quickly ascended from humble kitchen remodels to designing a showplace for Larry Ellison, the second-richest man in the world.

The walls of his conference room were covered with slick photographs of his architectural triumphs, along with a curious snapshot of a clunky old boat. He explained that he had bought a decommissioned Icelandic car ferry and he was going to dock it nearby in San Francisco and that he and his wife were actually going to live inside its 150-foot-long raw space as though it were a floating Manhattan loft.

Even Olle's architectural style fused the rival Napa and Sonoma personalities. His work had the spare, clean, airy feeling of refined minimalism, but he also liked to juxtapose modernist materials such as slick steel with rough volcanic stones quarried from the house's site or recycled wooden planks taken from abandoned old factories. He combined an elitist urban sophistication with environmental sensitivity.

As we stood in front of the wall of his conference room, I looked longingly at the dreamlike photographs of the Benioff pool overlooking Napa's twilight and fog.

"The agony we went through with Marc's house!" Olle exclaimed. "The *agony*! And then he went and sold it!"

Another photo display was labeled "Barnes Residence, Napa, CA, 2000." It showed a modernist jewel of a pool house in wood, glass, steel, and slate. Barnes was a young salesman for a printing company. A few years earlier, one of his clients was a technology venture called Cisco Systems. Barnes had gotten stock in Cisco. By his early thirties he was wealthy enough to commission Olle to build him a Napa mansion and pool house. Olle had executed the smaller structure first. But now that the NASDAQ had crashed, Barnes couldn't afford to go through with the plans for the much larger main house.

The techno boys were indeed in retreat, but the food-and-wine elite in the Napa Valley were still enjoying their profits from a decade of extraordinary prosperity. Olle had finished a wine cave for Jean Phillips from Screaming Eagle and now he was designing a guest house for her, which was where she planned to live while Olle redid her main house. (Years earlier, Jean had hired Olle to remodel an old motorcycle-repair garage in St. Helena into offices for her real-estate brokerage.) And Olle had built dramatic caves with a private tasting room for the Napa winery of Leslie Rudd, the chairman of Dean & DeLuca, which had done extremely well with its Manhattan-sized gourmet store in St. Helena.

The Napa Valley was like Hollywood: an efficient machine for finding whoever in the world had too much money at the time and taking it from them. They were forces for wealth redistribution. When the Japanese were flush in the eighties, they had succumbed to the aura of both places. So had the Silicon Valley moguls during their time in the nineties. And it seemed certain that future new-money crowds would follow.

I realized this during my second trip to the annual Napa Valley Wine Auction, in June 2001, when the devastation of the stock crash was still fresh. I went to lunch at the home of Naoko Dalla Valle, whose Maya was one of the two or three most prominent and sought-after of the famous cult wines. The lunch was a chance for rich outsiders to talk with the winemaker Mia Klein, an old hippie with long black hair that was going gray, who charged a $500-an-hour fee for her consulting services to vintners such as Naoko Dalla Valle.

Naoko lived near Auberge du Soleil in a Mediterranean-style villa on twenty acres in the foothills of the Vaca Mountains. At lunch we sat in the sun poolside, enjoying the requisite spectacular views of the valley while being served by the chefs and waiters of the Ritz-Carlton Hotel in San Francisco, who had come up specially for this meal. I was at a large round table with three couples who didn't know each other beforehand but realized that they were all in the oil and gas businesses. They were doing very well now that a fellow oil-man was president of the United States. For two hours they compared notes about all of the very backward and humid places they had lived, like Malaysia and Saudi Arabia and Texas and Louisiana. Later that year the most high-flying energy company, Enron, had its infamous collapse. I began to wonder whether attendance at the Napa Valley Wine Auction was a leading indicator of who in the world had too much funny money at that particular moment and needed to convert it into the most tangible and lasting asset—land in the most desirable of places—before it was too late.

THE STRANGEST EPILOGUE to my season in Sonoma was the unexpected fate of the free-roaming chickens. When the city council voted in June 2000 to bring the flock to the Plaza, its members decided to delay the return until late November, after the tourist season had ended. This way the birds wouldn't be chased and harassed for a while by out-of-town children who didn't know how to comport themselves around wildlife. The chickens could coexist peacefully with the locals for the quieter winter months and reestablish their reputation as peaceful symbols of Sonoma's rural tradition. And by delaying the reintroduction of the chickens until after the November election, the city council removed one divisive issue from what nonetheless proved to be a highly controversial and politicized time in the life of the town.

And so, at two in the afternoon on Friday, November 24—ironically, the day after Thanksgiving, that holiday glorifying the consumption of wild poultry by predatory humans—the farmer Bob Cannard, Sr., ceremoniously released a dozen hens onto the Plaza in front of a happy crowd of three dozen chicken enthusiasts.

But ten days later, a city parks employee came to work on a Monday morning and found four of the birds dead. They were brutally mutilated. (A fifth bird, badly injured, was taken to a nearby farm to recuperate.) An investigation placed the probable time of death between two and four in the morning. The leading theory maintained that the chickens were attacked by large dogs. Conspiracy theorists, skeptical that the attack could have been caused by negligence—dogs had never before killed Plaza birds in their long history there—speculated that perhaps it was a revenge killing by one of the many opponents of the chickens, a vigilante act by a political loser. The perpetrator might have been a dog activist. Canines were not allowed on the eight-acre park grounds of the Plaza that chickens once again roamed freely. Other theorists, reasoning from the perspective of naturalists in a place that was still close to nature, thought the killers might have been nocturnal predators such as raccoons or skunks, or perhaps even hawks. But the chickens had not been eaten. The case remained an unsolved mystery.

Nonetheless, the threat to the remaining chickens was untenable. Bob Cannard removed the rest of the flock on December 5, and as of this writing there were no plans to attempt to bring back the birds that many locals loved.

The final blow to chicken fans came in the spring of 2002, when a Sonoma County Superior Court judge ruled that Jerry Marino, the intransigent owner of the Chicken Car Wash, had to help the city get rid of the dozens of feral chickens that lived around his facility and the vacant lot next door. The owners of the El Pueblo motel had complained that their guests couldn't sleep through the squawking. Residents of nearby condos and senior-citizen homes griped about stepping in chickenshit and fearing roosters. So the judge banished the chickens, with the token concession that Jerry

Marino could keep six birds if he built a pen to contain them. And the pen had to be covered fully so the headlights of coming cars wouldn't provoke the birds into rambunctious squawking.

Sadly, inevitably, Sonoma was becoming like America.

THE BIGGEST MYSTERY that remained was why the dreaded glassy-winged sharpshooter hadn't devastated the Napa and Sonoma valleys as the newspapers and the speakers at the public forums and the coffeeshop prognosticators had all predicted. The fall harvests in 2000 and 2001 were untouched by the malicious insect. They were robust and highly profitable. The mood was so optimistic that Sonoma County's politicians, bowing to pressure from the environmentalists, declared that the government would only spray pesticides on private lands—"chemical trespass," it was called—as a "last resort" to fight an epidemic after first trying "organic alternatives" such as removing the deadly insects by hand.

As the new grape-growing season began in the spring of 2002, I decided to seek out the world's foremost authority on the glassy-winged sharpshooter and find out precisely what had happened and what to expect.

The leading expert was located conveniently right around the San Francisco Bay at the University of California at Berkeley. He was Dr. Alexander "Sandy" Purcell, a tenured professor of insect biology (and amateur home winemaker who had concocted about fifteen gallons that year). Even though he was officially on sabbatical, he was still working rather actively and he agreed to meet with me on the campus, which suggested that he was either a chronic workaholic or that the severity of the glassy-winged crisis had yet to subside.

Purcell's academic department was housed in a pre–World War II stone building, and the interior seemed stuck in the 1940s, as though it were a stage set for a scene early in one of the Indiana Jones movies when Harrison Ford is still a straight-laced bespectacled teacher. When I opened the door to Purcell's office (wooden frame and glazed glass with stenciled black lettering, as though he were a work-alone forties film noir detective), the professor was sitting behind his desk. He was tall and skinny and somewhat patrician in a crisp blue-striped white dress shirt and neat corduroy slacks. His office was overflowing with books and papers.

"Remember that in the movies, the evil professor always has a very clean office," he told me, "while the good professor's office is always messy."

Still, he seemed embarrassed enough by the disorder to take me down the hall so we could have our conversation in his unoccupied laboratory. I had expected a more high-tech-looking scientific milieu, something sleek and white and plastic, but the room was reminiscent of an old high-school chemistry lab with microscopes and test tubes.

Sandy Purcell, like so many people whose fate led them to the wine country, got there through an unlikely path with a little bit of luck and accident. He had worked in a lab as a teenager in Baton Rouge, Louisiana, but his real ambition was to fly. He graduated from the Air Force Academy in 1964 and spent six years as a captain and pilot in the service, which took him to Vietnam. He left the Air Force in 1970, hoping to return to civilian life as an airline pilot, but his timing was poor: The commercial carriers were beginning sweeping layoffs. So Sandy fell back on his skills in biology and went to California hoping to work in private agriculture. But then he found his own opportunity to live in paradise—for *free*! The University of California needed a graduate student to live gratis on idyllic Spring Mountain overlooking the Napa Valley while conducting some research about wine grapes. Sandy took the position, enrolling as a doctoral student.

The problem with growing grapes on Spring Mountain was Pierce's disease, the bacterial infection of the vines spread by the sharpshooter. At that point the glassy-winged species hadn't made it to California yet. The disease was spread mainly by a predecessor, the blue-green sharpshooter, which was much smaller and weaker and couldn't fly nearly as far or as fast or wreak havoc so quickly. Still, the blue-green had done great damage in the 1880s, when it wiped out grape growing in Los Angeles. Grapes had been a significant business there. The first Pierce's disease epidemic began in Anaheim, which was then a popular retirement place for Germans from San Francisco. It closed fifty wineries, though back then a winery was more like someone's backyard than a great plantation. Still, the insect was why Orange County in southern California became Orange County and not Grape County. It was why Anaheim's big tourist attraction became Disneyland rather than tasting rooms and picnics at fabulous wineries. The sharpshooter was also why wine grapes grew in so few places in the southeastern states, from Texas to Florida, even though their hot sunny summers and mild frost-free winters were otherwise well-suited for viticulture.

Sandy Purcell told me that Pierce's disease broke out in California's agricultural heartland, the Central Valley, in the 1920s and 1930s, and the threat was serious enough to provoke investigations by the University of California, the State of California, and the U.S. Department of Agriculture. But by the mid-1940s it became clear that less than one percent of the vines were harmed. The disease was a minor problem, a cost of doing business, not a catastrophe, and so hardly any significant research was conducted about it for twenty-five years. Then Sandy came along in the 1970s to Spring Mountain Road in Napa, one of the same places that the original researcher Newton Pierce had described when he first studied the disease a century earlier, and sure enough "it was in the damned same place out there on the vines," he told me.

Purcell's research became well-known within the narrow priesthood of his academic field, but his more public fame didn't come until the arrival of the glassy-winged sharpshooter near the vineyards of southern California in the 1990s. The glassy-winged wasn't a new thing, actually. It was a common bug in Louisiana when Pur-

cell was growing up there in the 1950s. When the grown-up Purcell would go back to his mother's backyard in Baton Rouge, he
could watch glassy-winged sharpshooters move from one orna-
mental plant to three others in a single day. Somehow, though, the
glassy-winged had migrated from the southeast to the west, probably taken inadvertently by a truck carrying houseplants to a store.

The devastation to the grapes was astonishingly quick. The
glassy-winged was discovered in the Temecula Valley in southern
California in 1989 and by the following year the vineyards there
were nearly wiped out. The blue-green had worked its damage
slowly but surely. The glassy-winged worked with brutal swiftness.

"It's evolution in action right before our eyes," Purcell said.

The glassy-winged's effect was exponential rather than linear,
meaning it just gained momentum and took off.

"Our conservative model shows that a very small number of
glassy-winged sharpshooters can spread the disease dramatically,"
Purcell said. "It doesn't take a whole lot of bugs to do a helluva lot
of damage."

So, I asked, what was going to happen in Napa and Sonoma?

"I'm optimistic," he said softly, but then he was very careful to
hedge that judgment. "In science, 'expert opinion' means you don't
know so you have to 'ask an expert.' Most of my predictions have
been wrong. Unfortunately the glassy-winged sharpshooter turned
out to be much worse than I thought it would be. In Temecula I
thought five to six years but the vineyards went down in one year."
The problem was partially the selfishness and greed of the growers:
"In Temecula people were reluctant to pull out the diseased vines,"
which would have inhibited the bug from spreading the infection.
"They wanted to get *one more crop* out of them."

In southern California the vintners had underestimated the
threat. "Denial is the first almost knee-jerk response to Pierce's
disease," he told me. "People said, 'Oh we'll take care of it.' But
Pierce's disease is a great humbler."

After the Temecula debacle, Purcell had thought it was too late to save the Napa and Sonoma valleys, even with efforts for a quarantine. But nonetheless the vintners pushed the government into conducting impressively close inspections of all the outside plants that were coming into the counties for sale at garden centers and other retail stores, and that had succeeded—so far at least—in keeping out the glassy-winged. The creatures had turned up in suburbs in the eastern and southern parts of the Bay Area but only one had made it north to Sonoma and it was caught by inspectors before it could get from the Home Depot into the prime vineyards.

"The government's job is to 'think the unthinkable' about the glassy-winged sharpshooter crisis," Purcell said. "Have public debates and handwringing and calculations far in advance before it happens. Controversy has arisen in Sonoma County mainly because of the public health risk. If someone uses the word 'nerve toxins,' you know that they're against insecticides. But you would only need intensive use over small acreages for a short time to eradicate incipient population instead of treating much larger acreages indefinitely into the future. And we're spending a lot of money on prevention. It's like watching a fire. After a while if the fire is too big, you just have to watch it burn."

I asked about ways of combating the bug without pesticides. Purcell said that nature played a role. He had discovered that for some unknown reason, freezing winter temperatures could completely cure a vine that had been infected during the summer growing season. That's why Georgia's farmers could raise wine grapes so long as their plots were at least twelve hundred feet above sea level, where the frost set. Washington State and Oregon had cold enough winter temperatures so their grape growers didn't have to worry about the disease. But Napa and Sonoma were in a climactic middle zone that left them vulnerable, so that one year out of ten could be warm enough to be catastrophic, Purcell said.

One out of ten. No business could survive decimation once a decade, especially vineyards, where it took four to five years for a newly planted vine to grow to maturity.

What about the solution that many of the environmental activists were proposing: Importing the species of wasps that were natural predators of the glassy-winged?

"They can knock the number of glassy-winged sharpshooters down from five thousand in a citrus tree host to five hundred," Purcell said. "And if it's five hundred and *then* you do other things like treat them with insecticides, that works okay. That's 'integrated pest management,' but it isn't the same thing as organic farming. Some wags call it 'integrated pesticide management.' "

Then the conversation became really frightening.

"It may actually come down to having *fences* to keep these out."

Fences? In the famously scenic *Napa Valley*!

Yes, fences. Purcell had a photograph of the largest vineyard in Florida, an experimental site that contained a mere two acres protected from the sharpshooters by fences.

How high would the fences have to be?

"Pretty damn high," he said. "When the sharpshooters hit a fence, they fly higher. You would need some way to stop them from going over the top. And from trees they can fly high! Envision a window-screen type fence thirty feet tall surrounding the perimeter of a vineyard. It would complete nullify the tourist ambiance because vineyards would come to be so ugly."

What about breeding wine grapes to become resistant to the bug?

"Ten to fifteen years is a realistic goal for resistant table grapes and raisins," he said. "For premium grapes? As they say in New York, fuhgeddaboutit. Maybe if it's 'ruby red' as opposed to cabernet sauvignon."

He rolled his eyes.

And what about genetic engineering?

"Is it possible to slip a couple of genes into cabernet sauvignon? That's the hype," he said. "But a lot of people in Europe and the United States won't drink it if it's genetically engineered. And with conventional breeding it's going to be very hard to come up with resistant wine grapes.

"I've seen the future and it isn't pretty. I went to Parras in the Sierra Madre in Mexico, a sixteenth-century hacienda, five thousand feet high, a desert plateau. Grapes have been grown there continuously since 1596, the longest in the Western Hemisphere. And do they have Pierce's disease? Boy, do they. A little creek full of glassy-winged sharpshooters. The only wine grape they can grow is lenoir. That's what they grow in Texas for red sherry and brandy."

And surely no one was going to visit the Napa Valley for mediocre sherry. But as Purcell continued, he speculated that Napa and Sonoma were just the first unlucky stop on the glassy-winged's tour of the world's greatest wine regions.

"There's a very distinct possibility that it could affect Mediterranean Europe and north Africa. Anywhere you can keep a backyard orange tree alive for twenty years, this thing will survive. And there are orange trees in Provence and the Po Valley.

"A couple of years ago I got e-mail from Macedonia to confirm that Pierce's disease occurs in grapes there. And Pierce's disease should be very rare there in Kosovo because of the climate. Can you imagine if it gets to a more favorable climate? Can you imagine the cradle of viticulture, Greece, not having any viticulture? I've asked, why hasn't this gotten to Europe? I'm giving a talk in Europe next week. Europe has a very common sharpshooter there naturally. And if they get the glassy-winged sharpshooter from North or South America, they're in trouble just as we are. Denial is the first step. It's like seeing rattlesnakes in a schoolyard. People say, 'It's in Kosovo? That's not Italy's problem. And there's a war there in Kosovo!' I can tell you for sure if it gets out of there, all bets are off. Greece, Italy, and southern France all have the right climate."

I imagined thousands of years of history and tradition, such a vital part of Western culture, finally terminated. And I decided it was a very good idea to build up my wine cellar.

"In Napa, we're not talking two or three years to total obliteration," he concluded, a good-natured prophet of doom. "It's going to take longer. But it will be inevitable."

And that was even *with* the early spraying of pesticides. And so, *without* chemicals, would Sonoma have any chance? Now that the local activists were so victorious, the northern California wine country seemed even more vulnerable to these doomsday scenarios. The final irony was that the movement that had saved Sonoma's culture and natural beauty for the coming generation also raised the risk of its demise.

ACKNOWLEDGMENTS

I'M GRATEFUL TO my generous hosts in Sonoma and Napa—Celia Canfield, David Applebaum, Ann Winblad, and Marc Benioff—and I apologize for repaying their hospitality with the ingratitude of subjecting their lifestyles to scrutiny. I've liked and admired all of them for many years, and I hope they'll view their treatment here as affectionate.

Many thanks to the Sonomans who accepted me into their small community with such warmth and camaraderie even though my project threatened to expose their private lives and bitter rivalries to an international audience. I'm particularly indebted to the members of the Yes Group—including Tom Whitworth, Jeri Lynn Chandler, Ditty Vella, Gary Edwards, Ken Brown, Joe Costello, and Dave Williams—and the bibliophiles at my favorite local haunt, Readers' Books, especially Andy and Lilla Weinberger, Kathleen Caldwell, and Emma McMacken. Thanks as well to my neighbors in Sonoma, Brad and Sue Gross.

Much gratitude to John and April Stallcup and Jeff Schechtman in Napa for their humor, friendship, and insights. Thanks as well to Jean-Noel and Marketta Fourmeaux at Château Potelle, Charles Sawyer and Brad Warner at Sawyer Cellars, and Gil and Beth Nickel and Mary Grace at Far Niente for giving me a privileged look inside their superb Napa wineries and, in some cases, even letting me help a bit with their crushes.

Thanks to everyone mentioned in this story—it would be redundant to name them all again here—and to the many other people who offered their perspectives and extended their hospitality, including Kimberly Charles at Magnet Communications, Charlotte Milan at Clos du Val, Robert Brittan and Allison Simpson at Stag's Leap, and Bette and George Starke at Zinfandel House. Thanks to Tom Fuller and Monte Sander, benefactors of journalist-gourmands everywhere, for inviting us to the Napa Valley Wine Auction, and I hope that I'll always be welcomed back there.

In San Francisco I've been fortunate to have many friends who encouraged me even though this assignment was so ridiculously enviable that it could have incited their resentment. I would like especially to thank Katharine Mieszkowski, Shyamala Reddy, Andrew Nelson, Jack and Victoria Dougherty, Dorka Keehn, Mariví Lerdo de Tejada and those fabulous ballplayers, the Elucidators.

At Broadway Books, Gerry Howard believed in this story from the beginning, Suzanne Oaks provided valuable early advice, Kristine Puopolo thoughtfully shaped and guided the manuscript to completion, and David Drake and Alana Watkins strived energetically to help bring it to the world. Many thanks to my agents and guardians Suzanne Gluck and Sloan Harris for their care and wise counsel. And of course to my parents, Hal and Elaine, and my brother, Robert, for their constant support and love.

© ALLEN NOMURA

ABOUT THE AUTHOR

ALAN DEUTSCHMAN has been writing for top magazines since 1988. He has been a contributing editor at *Vanity Fair, GQ,* and *New York* magazine, and he was the Silicon Valley correspondent for *Fortune.* He is the author of the *Wall Street Journal* and *BusinessWeek* bestseller *The Second Coming of Steve Jobs.* He lives in San Francisco.